Small Stage Sets on Tour

by James Hull Miller

A practical guide to
portable stage sets

MERIWETHER PUBLISHING LTD.
Colorado Springs, Colorado

Meriwether Publishing Ltd., Publisher
P.O. Box 7710
Colorado Springs, CO 80933

Editor: Theodore Zapel, Arthur L. Zapel
Typesetting: Sharon Garlock
Cover design: Michelle Z. Gallardo

Library of Congress Cataloging-in-Publication Data

Miller, James Hull.

    Small stage sets on tour.
    1. Theaters—Stage-setting and scenery.
2. Amateur theater—Production and direction.
I. Title.
PN2091.S8M4956   1987   792'.025   87-42872
ISBN 0-916260-46-1

00051 40449

CONTENTS

PREFACE

All scenery reflects in some manner or another the methods by which it is moved and assembled for the stage; it is exceedingly rare to create scenic effects even for a single showing with no allowance for the most temporary of storage.

Thus scenery runs the gamut from dye painted backdrops folded into costume trunks to massive platform cubes swallowed up whole by 18-wheelers, from tinker-toy dowels in a USO footlocker to 5'-9" wide flats rolling out the end doorway of a railway baggage car. The time, the place and the need are all that really matter when the chips are down. I once inquired of an airline baggage handler the maximum size of a piece. He quickly replied, ". . . Anything we can get on the plane." But along the way you learn that you can't close a U-Haul™ door on a scenic piece that is as long as the specified length of the rig, and that inset wheels play havoc with a pack of flats. You also learn that not every theatre has a softwood floor, nor wants one for that matter. As the saying goes, "It's up for grabs."

My first experience handling scenery was in 1934. As a Freshman at Princeton (and in need of additional funds) I signed on with the Student Express, a campus trucking agency that moved anything and everything we could get our hands on. So one rainy morning I found myself in the railroad yards unloading scenery from a baggage car, scenery for a Broadway show on tour that was to play the McCarter Theatre that evening! This was the beginning of fifty years backstage, and I have been fascinated by the problems of transporting scenery ever since!

The Graff Ballet on Tour

Over the next five years I was active in both campus extracurricular theatres — the Triangle and the Intime; had gone on two of the Triangle Club's Christmas tours and had worked in four East Coast summer theatres. In all these projects some transportation was obviously involved and though the solutions were routine I was all the better for the practical experience. But in the fall of 1940 I received the phone call that precipitated me into the rigors of budget touring. The call was from a small ballet company booked on a middle-western tour, mostly playing colleges and civic clubs, with facilities ranging from city auditoriums to gymnasiums. Now a city auditorium can be a fully rigged proscenium theatre — it can

1

also be a small stage with a sloping floor upstairs in a turn-of-the-century town hall on the square.

The bus, of a vintage just short of the pasture, carried, in addition to costume racks, a dimmer board, cable and lights, and a couple of sacks of black velour curtains with tielines. Atop the bus and well lashed down were some bare flats and braces, lengths of threaded pipe and some sacks filled with hemp. With the hemp and pipes a rigging system could be fashioned for curtains where no rigging was present. And where there was no structure to which to attach the temporary rigging the empty flats could be erected and the loose velour thrown over them.

I recall one gymnasium in Missouri where no extension ladder was available. I tossed a rope over an open truss and shinnied up. Then, with assistance from below and inching along the lower chord of the truss, I rigged the pipes for the support of the black velour curtains.

The ballet tours were ultimately decimated by the gathering war clouds. The war over, I became a stage technician for university campus theatres where productions were "in house" classics with sets elaborately mounted and thereafter demolished for parts, save for the ubiqitous stock flats that were routinely scrubbed down and repainted. This world might have continued indefinitely had I not become fascinated with groups a little more adventurous, bringing fresh imagery to the "boondocks," so to speak, rather than staging at home in more comfortable surroundings.

Little by little I rejoined the world of roving players — not in the true sense of the Commedia dell' Arte but at least moving in and out of someone else's playing space when in town.

And so it was that I became a specialist in something that has been called, for want of a better title, "freestanding scenery," that is, scenery free of any commitment to a permanent rigging system, or a proscenium frame, or even a front curtain — features which might or might not be

2

available with a particular venue.

     Small Stage Sets on Tour *is a brief record of these years, not only of the technical aspects of the roving settings themselves but also a description of some of the places in which these settings landed. In view of the fact that my text* **Self-Supporting Scenery** *(and the accompanying film strip) and* **Stage Lighting in the Boondocks** *are available, emphasis is more on an overview of the possibilities of the stagecraft rather than details down to the "nth" degree.* ***Small Stage Sets on Tour*** *is written in the conversational style. It is not my intention to replace or reduplicate the basic text* **Self-Supporting Scenery***; rather to enlarge upon it from the perspective of compact travel and speedy setup.*

James Hull Miller

Section I:
PORTABLE STAGE SETS

Chapter 1:

Folding Screens

One of the more frustrating things about touring is the matter of entrances and exits: whence the actors come and wither they go when they are not needed.

This may involve little more than masking a doorway in a classroom (as suggested above) all the way to a not-too-distant experience with the ill-fated New Orleans World's Fair where a friend of mine and his playmakers had to share an open platform stage in a concert tent with a series of rock groups. For these, and hundreds of similar situations, self-supporting screens that can be both quickly deployed and as quickly removed will prove to be real lifesavers.

Now there are folding screens and folding screens — the variety seems endless. But to be truly useful the panels of a set of folding screens should fold either way. In the hardware line there is only one type of hinge that accomplishes this — the dressing-room screen hinge, but a notoriously weak hinge. There is also the problem of the open crack, inevitable with any metal hinge because of the metal being bent around the pin. In conventional stagecraft this crack can be masked by glueing on strips of muslin, often called "dutchmans." But of course this is a one-way, inward folding affair. To get relief from inward folding the vertical edges of some panels can be mitered to a preset angle and then rear-hinged, that is, if the hinges are mounted atop any plywood strapping for a complete fold-down. Still, the desired flexibility is not achieved.

It took me years to realize that the only crack-free, fully flexible folding device is the ancient Korean "paper" hinge found on many oriental screens, the hinge flaps being made of the same paper as the art work covering the screen frame — although cloth can be substituted for the paper.

If I were to choose the single most useful piece of scenery from my experience it would be a folding screen with fully reversible oriental flap hinging. Such a unit provides both masking and decoration and, properly arranged, it is inherently self-supporting.

The above sketch suggests a situation in which a folding screen unit of four panels has been arranged in a room several feet from a doorway. This screen (1) masks the doorway, (2) furnishes a sheltered space for small "off-stage" props, (3) serves as a surface for background decor (in this case, that of a restaurant) and (4) provides some motivation for dramatic movement: the way to the kitchen is obviously to the right around the screen while the customers could have entered from the left around the other end of the screen.

There is one additional requirement for fully reversible folding screen sets: frames so constructed that they are flush on *both* sides! Not a big thing, really . . . but ask the average scene technician for a frame that is flush on both sides and you would think a trip to the moon had been proposed — though it has not been too many years since such construction was routine — for instance, the flats which ran in the nineteenth century stage "grooves."

The only problem for the beginning technician is that "clean" frames are a must if the screens are to be fully "reversible," that is, the structural frames must be flush on *both* sides, unlike most theatrical "flats" whose parts are joined by ¼" plywood strapping to the rear. The drawing which follows shows my own solution for structuring a "clean" frame.

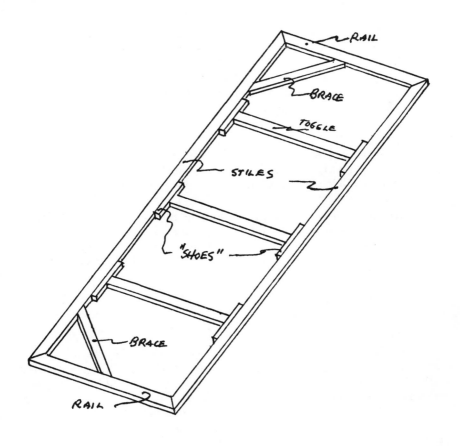

The toggles, rails and stiles are of ¾"x1-¾" strips ripped from soft pine "shelving." In a pinch "1x2" furring strips can be used but the slightly wider batten is preferable. The corner miters are carefully cross-nailed and the toggles are inserted by using "shoes" which are first nailed to the toggles and then in turn to the stiles. It is important that the frames be rectangular, that is, properly "squared up" prior to securing the braces.

However, one does not have to get into "shoe-type" joints for the simpler example shown here. This frame can be accomplished with some "1x2s" carefully assembled with nails and glue.

A workbench and layout table can be made with a sheet of ¾" by 4'x8' plywood laid on some sawhorses. For tools you will need a miter box of some sort, a backsaw, a drill with assorted bits, a one-inch chisel, four clamps, a hammer and a framing square. For materials — some muslin, Elmer's™ glue and nails.

There is a better way to go about making these frames but more sophisticated tools are required and I will describe these methods later. For now the important thing is to get this particular screen set built for purposes of further discussion.

A good size for a starter is a panel 3' by 7' — the 7' being essential in order to mask off the doorway, usually dimensioned for a 6'-8" standard door. With the saw and chisel make insets about ½" deep for the toggles. Drill "passing" holes for the joints. During assembly the battens can be held firm by clamping.

A simple covering for a beginner will be unbleached muslin, secured by coating the rails and stiles *only* with a thin coating of Elmer's™ glue. Make sure the muslin is pulled taut, then trim before the glue is completely dry. After the glue has dried the surface can be primed for scene

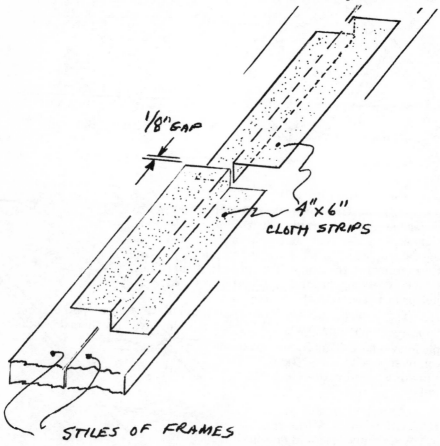

⅛" GAP

4" x 6" CLOTH STRIPS

STILES OF FRAMES

10

painting by brushing on a size made up of equal amounts of water and Elmer's™ glue.

Cover *both* sides of the frames with muslin. Then cut 4" wide strips of muslin about an inch short of the height. Divide by folding and refolding a strip so that pieces 6" long can be cut for the hinge flaps.

The frames are joined by these 4"x6" strips of muslin. A portion of each strip is first glued to the face of one stile, then later it is passed through the joint and glued to the underside of the other stile. First place the screens together and alongside of one another. Allow a slight gap between the hinges. The final flap will probably have to be custom cut. Now gently pull the frames apart to make sure that each flap is glued only to the proper stile. Let dry. Then turn the screens over and gradually move them together while bringing up the loose ends of the flaps through the common joint. Now glue the loose ends to the opposite stiles.

The steps for gluing the cloth flap hinge are reviewed again here:

1. Lay the panels to be joined alongside one another and glue down the flaps alternately as shown, leaving about ⅛" between the flaps.

2. Gently separate the panels to be sure that each hinge piece is attached only to the correct panel.

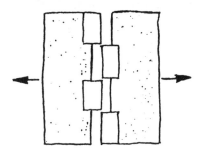

3. When the glue is dry, turn the panels over. Place a pair of them, just touching, in an inverted "V" position, then slowly lay them down flat

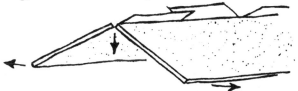

in such a way that the free ends of the hinge flaps come up through the joint.

4.   Close the joint tightly. Carefully glue down the flaps, making sure no slack is left but not pulling so hard that the panels are misaligned. Repeat until all panels are assembled into the screen set. The screens are now ready for painting and decoration.

The cloth flap hinge is also useful for joining kraft honeycomb core panels (International Honeycomb Corp., Chicago area . . . "Hexcel" is a trade name for this product). However, it will be necessary to firm up the corners and glue in little wooden blocks as shown. The preparation for these blocks is best done in a shop equipped with a table and possibly a band saw.

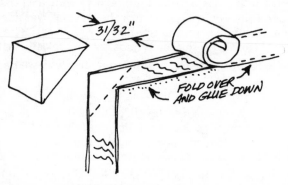

Strengthwise, the hinge flaps could even be made out of heavy kraft paper (60 lb. or more), but I do not recommend it because there is insufficient play with paper for the panels to settle properly on an uneven floor whereas muslin flaps have sufficient elasticity or "give."

A Proper Shop

Mention has been made of a proper worktable and two pieces of woodworking equipment: a table saw and a band saw. Unfortunately, without these items a great many of the stagecraft woodworking techniques in this book will become so time-consuming as to be not worth the trouble.

Typical saws are shown on the following page. The worktable should be sturdily made of a framework of 2x10s with intermediate members on 16" centers, and set on legs for an overall height of 29". The surface should be of 1x12" *soft* pine boards secured with recessed finishing nails. The soft pine is for temporary nailing to secure frames while fitting and to receive the ends of nails during the construction of lap-jointed frames for steps and platforms. The countersunk holding nails permit the use of a stencil knife without fouling its cutting edge. The worktable should be of a minimum area of 5x9 feet to a maximum of 6x12 feet. One should be able to walk completely around it.

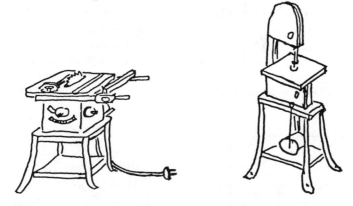

Above, a 9" tilting arbor table saw, and at right, a 14" band saw.

The need for these tools and layout table will become all too apparent very shortly. Folding archway sets such as that shown below will require some very sophisticated techniques. However, for the time being some fun things like the pavilion at right can be attempted with many materials using the glued-on cloth flap hinge.

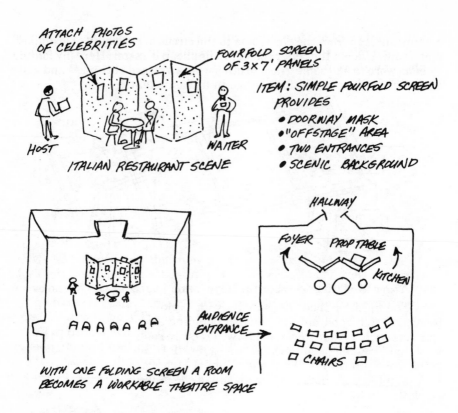

ATTACH PHOTOS OF CELEBRITIES

FOURFOLD SCREEN OF 3 X 7' PANELS

ITEM: SIMPLE FOURFOLD SCREEN PROVIDES
- DOORWAY MASK
- "OFFSTAGE" AREA
- TWO ENTRANCES
- SCENIC BACKGROUND

HOST

WAITER

ITALIAN RESTAURANT SCENE

WITH ONE FOLDING SCREEN A ROOM BECOMES A WORKABLE THEATRE SPACE

AUDIENCE ENTRANCE→

HALLWAY

FOYER   PROP TABLE

KITCHEN

CHAIRS

The above illustration shows a folding screen in action in a typical classroom situation. Examples from my own experience are legion but the most interesting instance of "instant" scenery took place at Portland State University in the late 1960s. The Art Department furnished both band and table saws and had proper worktables constructed. The basic folding screen, with both opaque and archway panels, was the most popular item. In fact, just two days into the five-day workshop the teachers requested that further demonstrations be suspended in favor of the manufacture of folding screens for their classrooms. So I turned my efforts towards the resupply of materials and supervision. "How many are you going to build?" I asked, and one teacher replied, "As many as I can fit into my classroom closet."

A Saga of Art and Bankruptcy

Now to return to the aforementioned New Orleans' World's Fair in

14

a quantum leap from the classroom to the circus atmosphere of grandiose plans sailing down the roller coaster to financial disaster! Here my folding screens were to add some grace to otherwise awkward entrances and exits to and from an open platform stage in a plastic tent.

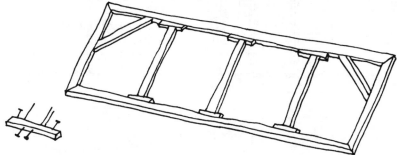

The screen sets were 12' high, in fourfolds with panels 50" wide. The frames were made of ¾" x 1-¾" pine (custom ripped on the table saw). Note also that the toggles have been joined to the stiles by an adapter or "shoe" made of ¾" x ¾" strips of wood, also prepared on the table saw. The frames were then covered on one side only with Veltex℠, the trade name for a flameproofed 100% cotton teasled velour from Valley Forge Fabrics of New York City. Reversible cloth flap hinging was by Veltex℠ strips blind tacked on the face side through narrow strips of picture mattboard in the manner of upholstery blind-tacking.

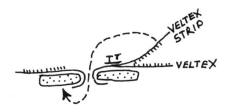

The screens were manufactured in my studio, the Arts Lab, in northern Louisiana, and New Orleans was some 300 miles away. But I had only to pick up the morning newspaper to know that the meagre advance I had received for materials and labor would be the last money I would ever see from the Crescent City for this project, so there was nought to do but to get them delivered at the lowest possible cost! I encased the screens, all 24 panels (in six sets of fourfolds) in a large plastic tarp and laced the bundle atop my car.

The trip took the better part of two days, crawling along byways at a top speed of 30 miles per hour, with frequent stops to rearrange and retie the load after airblasts from each passing truck and 18-wheeler. But once there, the tradition of small stage sets on tour was back on track, with deployment instantaneous!

15

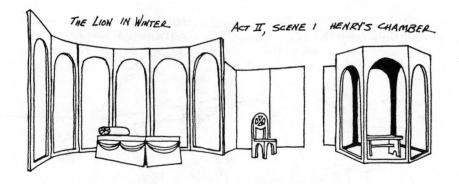

Arch Folds

There is probably nothing more useful (and easily transportable) than flat-framed arch panels using reversible cloth flap hinges. Stage movement is enhanced and accessorization is seemingly endless. Some years ago Paul Ebert of the Oak Ridge Community Playhouse in Tennessee not only built a set for the *Lion in Winter* out of the folding screens shown on this page but he also built a "flexible cyclorama" out of 3x14' fourfolds as shown on the plan on the following page. A crew of eight, black clad, handled the screens and props, working under dim backlight and in full view of the audience. The shifts took anywhere from one-half to one minute apiece. (Further details will be found in my book *Self-Supporting Scenery.*)

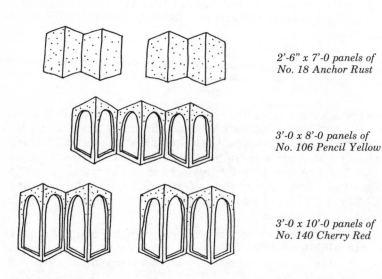

2'-6" x 7'-0 panels of
No. 18 Anchor Rust

3'-0 x 8'-0 panels of
No. 106 Pencil Yellow

3'-0 x 10'-0 panels of
No. 140 Cherry Red

Sketches on this page by Dan Hanley

16

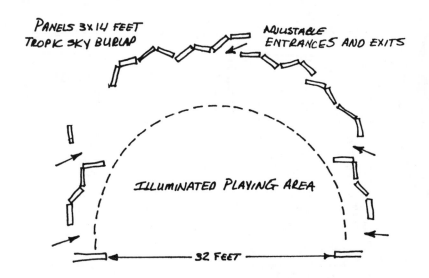

PANELS 3X14 FEET
TROPIC SKY BURLAP

ADJUSTABLE
ENTRANCES AND EXITS

ILLUMINATED PLAYING AREA

32 FEET

Profile

By this time, the reader has become aware (perhaps painfully so) that sets isolated in space bring with it a style of design which, regardless of its internal detail, shares one thing in common with sculpture: profile (or silhouette). By intention, the scenic object is *unframed* and therefore its perimeter is known and must possess esthetic validity.

The folding screen below was built during a workshop in free-standing scenery and was later employed in a lighting demonstration for the chapel scene in *Hamlet*.

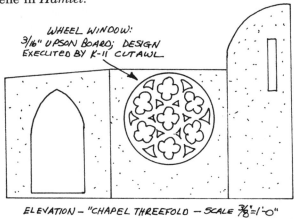

WHEEL WINDOW:
3/16" UPSON BOARD; DESIGN
EXECUTED BY K-II CUTAWL

ELEVATION — "CHAPEL THREEFOLD — SCALE 3/8"=1'-0"

ASSEMBLE THE THREE SCREENS
BY REVERSIBLE CLOTH FLAP HINGES.
EXPERIMENT WITH
ARRANGEMENTS.

17

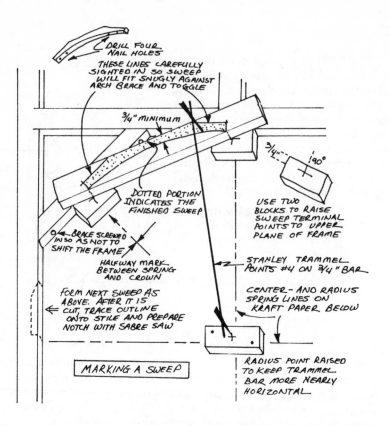

DRILL FOUR
NAIL HOLES

THESE LINES CAREFULLY
SIGHTED IN SO SWEEP
WILL FIT SNUGLY AGAINST
ARCH BRACE AND TOGGLE

3/4" minimum

DOTTED PORTION
INDICATES THE
FINISHED SWEEP

3/4"   90°

USE TWO
BLOCKS TO RAISE
SWEEP TERMINAL
POINTS TO UPPER
PLANE OF FRAME

BRACE SCREWED
IN SO AS NOT TO
SHIFT THE FRAME

HALFWAY MARK
BETWEEN SPRING
AND CROWN

FORM NEXT SWEEP AS
ABOVE. AFTER IT IS
CUT, TRACE OUTLINE
ONTO STILE AND PREPARE
NOTCH WITH SABRE SAW

STANLEY TRAMMEL
POINTS #4 ON 3/4" BAR

CENTER- AND RADIUS
SPRING LINES ON
KRAFT PAPER BELOW

RADIUS POINT RAISED
TO KEEP TRAMMEL
BAR MORE NEARLY
HORIZONTAL

MARKING A SWEEP

It is not often that a technical writer lays aside the mask of scientific anonymity and addresses himself directly to the reader in anecdotal style — but there is a time and place for everything, and now is the time to confess that nothing I have ever done has been as controversial as my way of making the arch for a "flush-on-both-sides" flat-folding frame. It has been resisted on both sides of the Atlantic and alternative schemes to the above are as numerous as April showers in spring. Yet none has proven as effective, though I await with anticipation and pleasure a successful counter proposal. The difficulties address the matters of weight, strength and the attachment of fabrics by lightweight staples. Nor are precut arch sweeps as easily seated as are custom-designed ones.

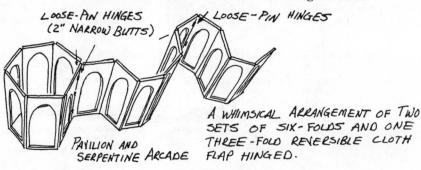

LOOSE-PIN HINGES
(2" NARROW BUTTS)

LOOSE-PIN HINGES

PAVILION AND
SERPENTINE ARCADE

A WHIMSICAL ARRANGEMENT OF TWO
SETS OF SIX-FOLDS AND ONE
THREE-FOLD REVERSIBLE CLOTH
FLAP HINGED.

The cloth flap hinge is an incredibly strong device, so sturdy it is still used on the rudders and ailerons of light aircraft. And so it was that I used this device on a set of open tracery arches soaring to an overall height of 18' for a Christmas pageant in a Houston church. The wood framework of this structure is detailed in my book *Self-Supporting Scenery*.

Again, delivery was atop my Pontiac Catalina whose overall length is all of 18'-6". And in this instance cruising speed was not a critical factor.

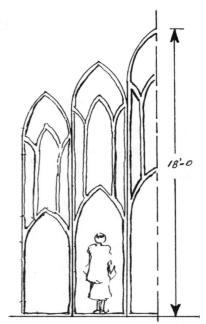

Other Considerations

One matter not yet discussed is the visual effect of the open joint on alternate foldings in a serpentive screen. First, an open joint must be distinguished from that of a crack that is caused by the offset action of a metal hinge. There you see through a crack — here you cannot see through an open joint. Frankly, the open joint does not bother me because there are usually partial shadows created. And where textured fabrics are employed the problem virtually disappears.

My first folding screens were covered and hinged with burlap, both natural and dyed. I have not mentioned this before for several reasons: involved is a more difficult assembly technique — stapling rather than gluing; unlike Veltex™ (and to some degree painted muslin) it is not light-proof and requires an opaque undersurface such as heavy kraft paper, not to mention flameproofing which deteriorates both fabric and dyes.

Offsetting these topical disadvantages are superior texture, minimal decor by "drybrushing," and the natural richness of dyes over painting. There is nothing that can match the visual impression of textured, dyed fabrics under stage lights.

Another advantage of self-supporting screens has to do with stage movement to the rear, no space being given over to the placement of stage braces or jacks. The masked area is *totally* usable.

19

The Case of the Rolling Blinds

"Elementary, my dear Watson!" is easily spoken when the solution has become apparent. But one of the most difficult challenges I have ever faced involved a countryside for the race of the tortoise and the hare and the need for a set solution that would "fly," *literally* speaking.

In the early 1970s the Everyman Players scheduled a European tour with this children's classic. The problem to be solved was the devising of some sort of scenery which could accompany the actors as *personal* baggage since separate shipment by air freight was economically out of the question.

Some years back I had need for a quick fence for my dog, so I went by Sears for one of those wire-woven picket fences that are usually secured to poles set in the ground. Only this time I was in a hurry and since the roll contained more fence than I needed, I discovered that, with sufficient undulations, the fence stood up very well by itself and the dog was sufficiently impressed by his new restriction to remain within it. So I put the poles aside and merely secured both ends.

When I learned of the scenic problem for *The Great Cross-Country Race* I immediately thought of the fence, and set about finding some sort of materials which would work in the same manner. After fiddling around with picture wire and slats I hit upon some old rolling blinds, the kind that roll up and down across verandas. Upended and profiled along the tops, sets of these "undulations" offered many fascinating entrances and exits. The scenic artist glued on narrow strips of colored felt, creating rich mosaics for the woodland scenes. Then the tightly rolled up blinds were stuffed into custom-made canvas sacks resembling so many oversize golf bags. An arrangement had been made with Air Italia and when these went down the personal baggage chute the mission was accomplished. For added stability some floor plates and shelf brackets, as well as accessory trims, went along in footlockers.

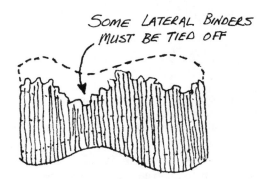

SOME LATERAL BINDERS
MUST BE TIED OFF

Where shipping space is not at a premium I have speeded up the stabilizing process by cutting large wooden discs and nailing one of them to the bottom of each of the serpentines. Weights are then placed on the discs.

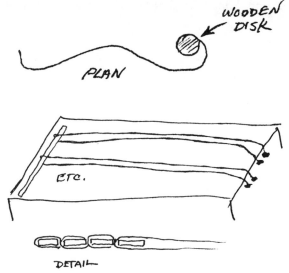

WOODEN DISK

PLAN

ETC.

DETAIL

While the weaving of such blinds from scratch can be tedious, it is not impossible. Then, any desired slats can be used. On a large work table secure the bights of double lines of strings by temporarily nailing down the top slat. Attach the ends of the strings to weights and let them hang over the work table, thus maintaining tension while the slats are worked in. Study a rolling blind and observe the offset patterns.

Screens As "Shelf" Items?

If folding screens are so useful, then why are they not on the market? The answer is not a simple one.

Part of the explanation lies in the nature of a market for them —they are most prized by the "have-nots," those who are *without* first class facilities, facilities which have adequate wing space and equipment for handling scenery on a vaster scale.

Another part of the answer lies in the fact that the manufacture of folding screens is labor heavy, that is, the value of market place labor far exceeds the cost of materials. With the "have-nots," of course, the labor is usually free.

Another part of the answer lies in the *ease* of customizing the screens for specific tasks in a labor-free market vs. the considerable amount of shipping and inventory that would be necessary to provide the same choice in necessarily pre-built models.

A final part of the answer lies in the maintenance factor when textured fabrics such as burlap are involved. Frequently the stapled fabrics go slack and must be tightened . . . or the dyes refreshed to counter sunlight, heat and dampness under poor storage conditions.

Chapter 2:

Walls, Steps & Platforms
(the mighty 2" C-clamp)

I got the idea for clamp-together scenery from early television scenery: those 4x8' panels quickly assembled by adding 1x4s around the perimeter and joined by bolting. In fact, many high school touring groups have made this technique into a fine art. Doors are no problem: with some flat battens added, the piece removed becomes the door. And there is such a variety of 4x8' panels in discount lumber yards that further decor is often unnecessary. True, turning corners requires a little ingenuity, and the threads of bolts may be damaged on tour. But, all in all, one is "off to the races" posthaste (especially if one doesn't have the customary shop power equipment).

I have, on occasion, made good use of this technique, but, in the main, I have preferred the C-clamp to the bolt — not only for flexibility but for the structuring of a far more sophisticated system of self-supporting scenery, one which has satisfied all my needs and expectations over the years.

During the 1950s I began experimenting with these new methods of lightweight construction for both wall slabs, steps and platforms either with the battens turned on-edge or lap-jointed. All such frames are so designed that units built with this construction can be joined to one another through clamping. On the two pages which follow sketches typical of this system are shown. The drawings are taken from photocopies of notes I made for a pamphlet titled *Freestanding Scenery* that was issued by the Hub Electric Co. in 1969.

Early on I discovered that 1x2"s were too narrow and that 1x3"s were too bulky. So I settled for strips that I ripped myself from 1x12"s. Using a blade with a narrow kerf I got six strips at approximately 1-$\frac{13}{16}$"

each. Those were the days of the full measure "1x12." Nowadays you can get five strips at that width plus a narrow strip for braces, cleats and other sundry purposes.

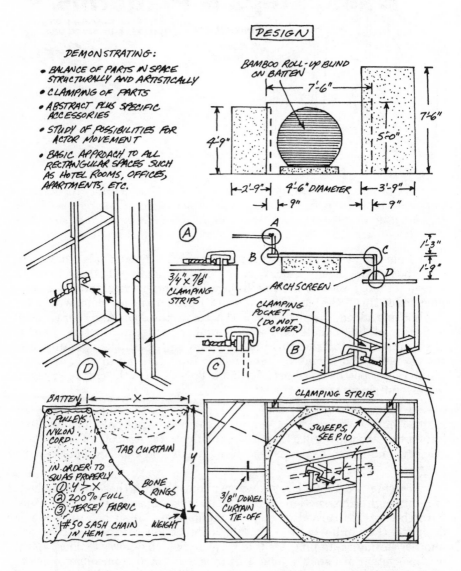

DESIGN

DEMONSTRATING:
- BALANCE OF PARTS IN SPACE STRUCTURALLY AND ARTISTICALLY
- CLAMPING OF PARTS
- ABSTRACT PLUS SPECIFIC ACCESSORIES
- STUDY OF POSSIBILITIES FOR ACTOR MOVEMENT
- BASIC APPROACH TO ALL RECTANGULAR SPACES SUCH AS HOTEL ROOMS, OFFICES, APARTMENTS, ETC.

BAMBOO ROLL-UP BLIND ON BATTEN

7'-6"
4'-9"
5'-0"
7'-6"

2'-9" 4'-6" DIAMETER 3'-9"
9" 9"

3/4" x 7/8" CLAMPING STRIPS

ARCH SCREEN

CLAMPING POCKET (DO NOT COVER)

1'-3"
1'-9"

BATTEN X
PULLEYS, NYLON CORD
TAB CURTAIN
IN ORDER TO SWAG PROPERLY
① 4 × X
② 200% FULL
③ JERSEY FABRIC
#50 SASH CHAIN IN HEM
BONE RINGS
WEIGHT
Y

CLAMPING STRIPS
SWEEPS, SEE P. 10
3/8" DOWEL CURTAIN TIE-OFF

With this system we have left the "1x2" behind — I used it only on page 9 so that a novice could get the framing going without having to resort to power tools. And for the classroom screen the "1x2" is OK. But a standard 2" C-clamp can't be seated properly (illustration B) if the batten strip is not at least 1-3/4" wide — either the clamp will protrude

24

beyond the plane of the facing if it is fabric or it will not fit in at all if the facing is solid.

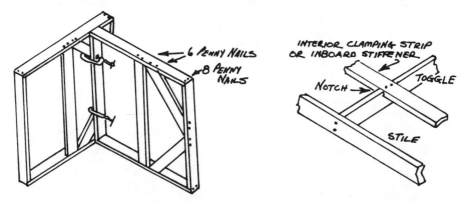

As can be seen from the illustrations this is not a difficult construction technique, save for the fabrication of archways. The arch facade for *Pilgrim's Progress* (see page 34) was constructed in this manner save that the battens were 2¼" wide and the facade subdivided into three sections and bolted rather than clamped together.

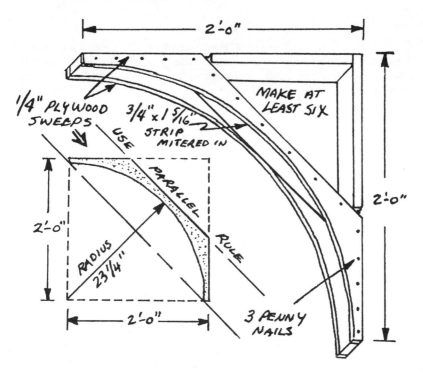

25

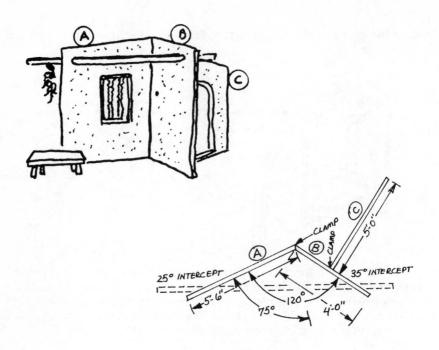

Above, left, is a clamp-together setting that is easily transported and quickly assembled. An important feature of clamp-together or "slab" construction is having both surfaces flush. In this example the rear face of (B) may have to be covered.

In the above set a two-fold "flat-framed" screen has been joined (by clamping) to an "on-edge," framed "slab" by means of a cloth-flap hinged folding strip. The slab is obviously double-covered.

Towers

At right is a concept drawing of the tower structure and full instructions are given in the text *Self-Supporting Scenery*. Towers are not particularly difficult to build. They are surfaced with panels of 3/16", 48" wide Upson™ board. A plan for one-fourth of a tower is shown below. A paper pattern is made, and after the top and bottom arcs are traced onto plywood the paper pattern can be cut up to form the segment patterns. Towers are structurally sturdy and the sections stack well for shipment.

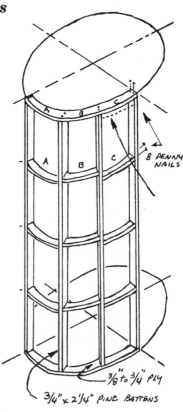

8 PENNY NAILS

3/8 to 3/4" PLY

3/4" x 2'/4" PINE BATTENS

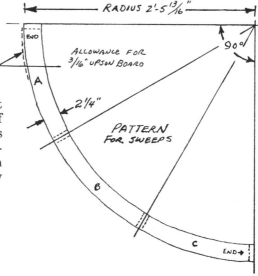

RADIUS 2'-5 13/16"

END

ALLOWANCE FOR 3/16" UPSON BOARD

90°

A

2 1/4"

PATTERN FOR SWEEPS

B

This pattern has been set up for a 48" wide sheet of Upson™ board. With this pattern a complete cylinder can be made, though three sections will satisfy most sightlines.

C

END

DRILL SCREW HOLE AND FINISH WITH 1/2" COUNTER-SINK — USE N°8 1 1/2" FLAT HEAD WOOD SCREW

STEPS WILL FORM BRACE IN THIS CASE

CLAMPING STRIP

1"x2" HOLES WILL TAKE 2" C CLAMP FOR CLAMP-TOGETHER SCENERY

3/4" PLYWOOD CAN BE SCREWED ON FOR EASY REMOVAL

CAN BE HINGED — LOOSE OR TIGHT PIN,

OR NAILED

CENTER FRAME

NOTE SAME FOR CENTER FRAME

FLUSH STRIP FOR COVERING

3/4" PLY

NAIL HERE BUT SCREW HERE

8 PENNY NAILS

6 PENNY NAILS

PINE BOARD

LAP-JOINT CONSTRUCTION
USING STANDARD 3/4" x 1-13/16" STOCK

HOW TO GET STARTED:

ALWAYS PLACE HORIZONTALS DIRECTLY ON SOFT PINE TABLE. THE FIRST TWO 6 PENNY LIGHT BOX CEMENT-COATED NAILS SHOULD HOLD OPPOSITE VERTICALS AND ALSO SECURE LOWER HORIZONTAL TO TABLE. TRUE UP WITH FRAMING SQUARE AND ADD SECOND NAILS. WHEN FRAME IS COMPLETED, PRY OFF WORK TABLE, TURN OVER, THEN HAMMER DOWN PROTRUDING NAILS.

GENERALLY SPEAKING, A FRAME IS REQUIRED EVERY THIRTY INCHES.

FRAMING SQUARE

Because the framing members are joined by light box cement (resin) coated nails, northern soft pine (ponderosa, spruce, etc.) is essential. A sturdy work table, topped with soft pine, is also essential. Firm, secure joints are necessary too. With the lap joints, the nail ends are hammered over. Air tackers will not work here. Nor will electrically driven screw nails. What we have here is the natural evolution of a system whose parts and techniques are completely interdependent. Substitutions create a domino effect which bring the whole system down. I realized that I had a whole new ballgame on my hands and I perceived that this game had to be played by the rules it had created. And the rules merge with the esthetics of design as well. Thus, with this book, I have the dual challenge of structure and design; design in terms of structure and structure in terms of design.

In conventional stagecraft the standard way to make up portable platforms that must be set up and knocked down from one scene to another is by the use of "parallels," rectangular folding frames onto which, when squared up, a cleated plywood top is placed. With the system shown here, the setup is designed to remain in place for the run of the performance and thus I can build more rigidity. So for platforms with lap-jointed frames I tight-pin the frames by pairs, then loose-pin hinge the pairs together with all hinges on the inside. This locks the frames in one position. However, frames can be lightly nailed together and later disassembled; so strong are these frames and so tightly do the overlapping parts fit. Finally, the plywood tops are screwed on for even greater rigidity.

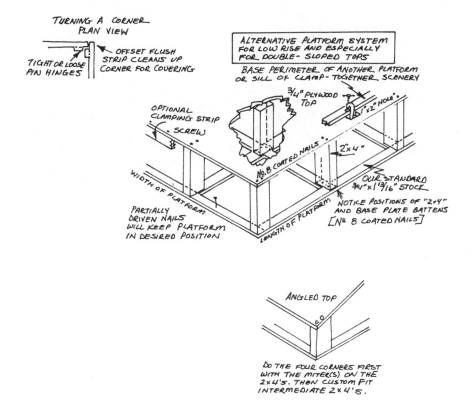

I generally start lap-jointed platform frames at a two-foot height. Lower platforms I make by the "stud" method as shown. The "stud" method is by far the best way to make sloped platforms.

While large platform areas are broken down into plywood tops and lap-jointed frames to reduce volume in transport, long runs of shallow steps and certain "core" interchanges are built as solid cubes. Shown here is such a core interchange suitable for interclamping between higher and lower units.

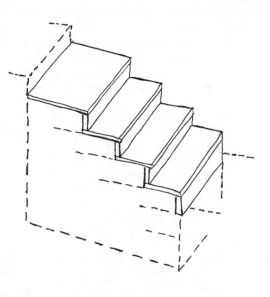

As my stockpile of platforms, ramps and steps began building up, the adaptability of the system became apparent, not only to myself but also to others, for borrowings increased to dramatic proportions. Of borrowings, the biggest crisis concerned a massive set of steps and platforms for the repertory staging of some operas where the locales were changed by props and costumes. After the performance, the set, together with some six dozen 2" C-clamps, disappeared into a storage area unknown to me — though not unknown to others, for I began seeing parts of it turning up all over town. And it was inevitable as rain that the day would come when the present owner wished to resurrect the set in its entirety — which sent me scurrying around trying to run down vital parts. Thereafter I stored the set against the pilfering of essential parts — though the continued borrowing of parts even under my supervision was like playing a giant game of jackstraws, for the desired parts always seemed to be on the bottom of the heap.

The reader will have to take my testimony on faith, for one of the

tragedies of working for the "have-nots" is the paucity of promotional material of a visual nature — the absence of a proper "portfolio," so to speak. Usually it is a matter of getting the job done with all possible dispatch from sketches on paper doilies and such during lunch.

Curved Stairs

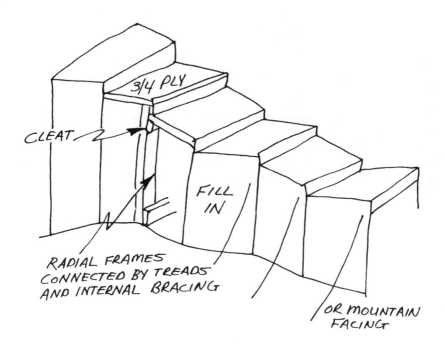

As far as I can remember the idea of making lap-jointed platform frames came from a set I built for *Peer Gynt* in the early 1940s, in which an irregular pathway ran up a mountainside. Here the shapes of the tread segments controlled the meanderings and each lap-jointed frame had a cleat which seated the rear of the tread. The same technique can be used for making spiral stairs, although lots of bracing is called for and the steps are not portable.

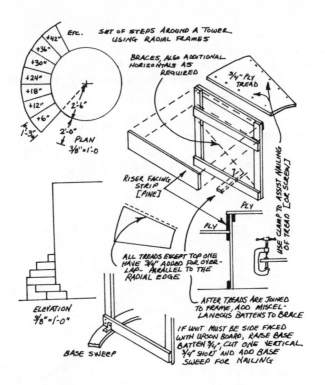

SET OF STEPS AROUND A TOWER USING RADIAL FRAMES

ETC.

+42"
+36"
+30"
+24"
+18"
+12"
+6"

2'-6"

1'-3"

2'-0"

PLAN
3/8"=1'-0

BRACES, ALSO ADDITIONAL HORIZONTALS AS REQUIRED

3/4" PLY TREAD

RISER FACING STRIP [PINE]

PLY

PLY

USE CLAMP TO ASSIST NAILING OF TREAD [OR SCREW]

ALL TREADS EXCEPT TOP ONE HAVE 3/4" ADDED FOR OVER-LAP- PARALLEL TO THE RADIAL EDGE

AFTER TREADS ARE JOINED TO FRAME, ADD MISCEL-LANEOUS BATTENS TO BRACE

IF UNIT MUST BE SIDE FACED WITH UPSON BOARD, RAISE BASE BATTEN 3/4", CUT ONE VERTICAL 3/4" SHORT AND ADD BASE SWEEP FOR NAILING

ELEVATION
3/8"=1'-0"

BASE SWEEP

In the years that followed I shifted the vertical structure from the common radial to dual side frames (or solid planes). This meant that a curved stair could be assembled from a series of highly portable *units* — units that not only could be compactly stacked for transport but, when assembled and interclamped, produced *instant* rigidity. Furthermore, there are many uses to which such a flexible system can be put. And when two sets of steps are fashioned in a mirror image parts can be interchanged and serpentines created.

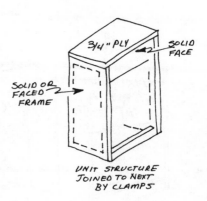

3/4" PLY

SOLID FACE

SOLID OR FACED FRAME

UNIT STRUCTURE JOINED TO NEXT BY CLAMPS

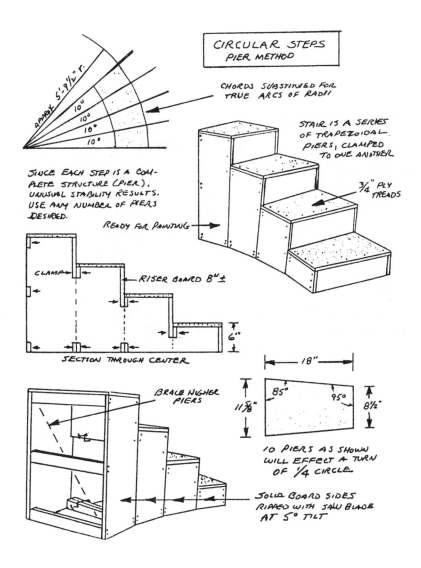

CIRCULAR STEPS
PIER METHOD

APPROX 5'-9½" R.

10°
10°
10°
10°

CHORDS SUBSTITUTED FOR TRUE ARCS OF RADII

STAIR IS A SERIES OF TRAPEZOIDAL PIERS, CLAMPED TO ONE ANOTHER

¾" PLY TREADS

SINCE EACH STEP IS A COMPLETE STRUCTURE (PIER), UNUSUAL STABILITY RESULTS. USE ANY NUMBER OF PIERS DESIRED.

READY FOR PAINTING

CLAMP

RISER BOARD 8" ±

6"

SECTION THROUGH CENTER

18"

85°   95°

11⅝"   8½"

10 PIERS AS SHOWN WILL EFFECT A TURN OF ¼ CIRCLE

BRACE HIGHER PIERS

SOLID BOARD SIDES RIPPED WITH SAW BLADE AT 5° TILT

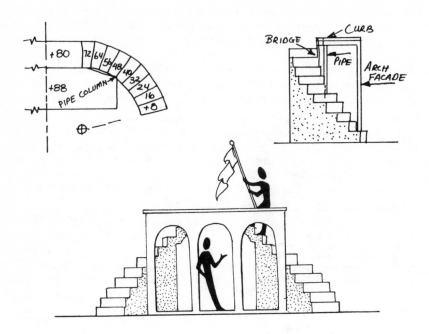

This concept of each step being a complete shaft or "pier" clamped to adjoining piers was applied to a set for *Pilgrim's Progress* for a tour of The Everyman Players. The steps led up to an arched pavilion with acting deck. The arched facade consisted of three arches constructed in the manner shown above, and then bolted together.

Both the players and the scenery went on a Greyhound bus since a tight schedule made it necessary for the scenery and the players to arrive at the same time. By removing some side windows and storing some of the seats the set could be accommodated in a portion of the aisle. The total space required for the entire set was 4' wide by 7½' long by 3½' high. Since the set could be assembled and dismantled with incredible speed, nightly performances could be scheduled in different locations, a noble example of "Small Stage Sets on Tour!" And for years afterwards the steps were useful in dozens of situations requiring quick vertical access of one sort or another.

The ELECTRA Ramp

Mention has been made of the slope stages which are still found in

"Turn of the Century" theatres — especially where the seating of a large portion of the audience on a flat floor permits other activities. A slope stage is a powerful visual device and one uniquely compatible with "wing-and-border" scenic effects — especially on the old "grooved" stages where flats (or "shutters," as they were called) could be slid off and on. [Overhead matching grooves secured the tops of the flats — these grooves were hinged offstage and could be raised to clear the space for other scenic effects.]

Though Realism and the "box set," along with revolving stages and other heavily dimensional scenic effects sounded the death knell for the formal slope stage, the dramatic experience of watching actors move on a tilted plane is not easily swept aside and directors will move mountains to obtain the effect. Fortunately, large-scale ramped platforms are not inherently difficult . . . even ones "on the move."

And move one we did, for a tour of the Everyman Players' version of *Electra!* The original set from which the tour version was taken consisted of a vast ramped platform in the shape of an isosceles triangle with a 32' wide base resting on the stage floor and rising at approximately 12° to an overall depth of 30 feet. For the road show, I reduced these dimensions to 24 x 20 feet at a 9° tilt, subdivided as shown on the plan to make the most of the standard ¾"x4'x8' plywood sheet.

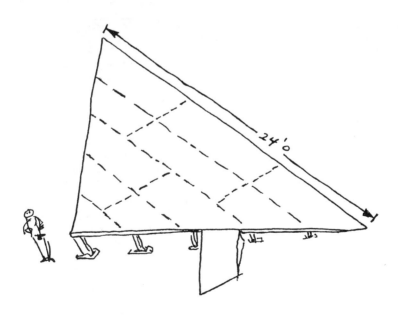

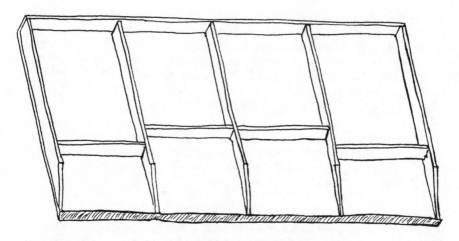

The sections were then ribbed with 1x4s at their perimeters and internally, usually laterally at 2' intervals or as required. The long edges of the panels contiguous to the floor had ½" of the ¾" thickness removed and this meant sending the panels through the table saw with the blade tilted at 9°, not an easy operation as shown in the action sketch.

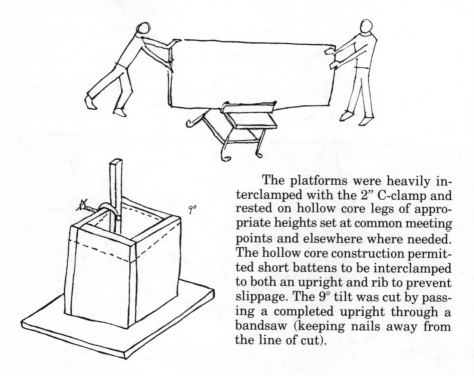

9°

The platforms were heavily interclamped with the 2" C-clamp and rested on hollow core legs of appropriate heights set at common meeting points and elsewhere where needed. The hollow core construction permitted short battens to be interclamped to both an upright and rib to prevent slippage. The 9° tilt was cut by passing a completed upright through a bandsaw (keeping nails away from the line of cut).

The ramp is made slip-proof by sand. Roll on a base coat of acrylic latex. Before it dries sprinkle lightly with sand. Then roll on another coat before drying. The platform, required about 1½ hours to assemble.

The *Electra* tour over, the ramped platform was stored intact against a rainy day — and rainy days were not long in coming. The Everyman Players used it again on tour, this time for *The Tempest,* with the platform reversed and pointed downstage, thus providing a ship's prow, a cave underneath, and a marvelous sense of "over the bluff" island terrain, with ample downstage acting areas to the side.

The ramp was then used for *Tell Pharoah,* a Black choral diatribe against "Whitey;" also the *The Dybbuk,* a 1930s classic of Jewish spirits exorcised; and still later for *Gianni Schicci,* the Italian operatic version of Ben Jonson's *Volpone.* A goodly part of the ramped platform found its way into the church as will be described in Chapter 4. Finally, the ramp went off to Dallas in a pickup truck where it was incorporated into a children's festival production of *Alice in Wonderland* in an outdoor park. Of course, in the wake of all these productions a considerable amount of furniture remained that was fit only for a 9° sloped surface. From an acoustical standpoint the siting for singers was superb.

Instruction for Constructing a Ramp

Previously the "stud" method was suggested for constructing ramps as well as low platforms. Shown here is a complete ramp. Properly constructed such structural stability to an adjoining unit deserves special mention.

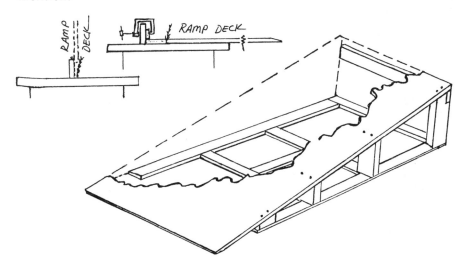

First, determine the ramp angle. Then bevel the ends as shown in the table saw operation sketch at the previous page, upper left. Next, prepare the side studs for the upper end of the ramp, allowing ¾" for the floor plate. Rip the clamping strip for the upper end and trace profiles to prepare the notches for the studs. Secure the clamping strip and studs. Place the side floor plate battens in tentative positions and mark for length. Also prepare the other side studs. Secure these studs, then turn the ramp over and secure the side floor plate battens. The studs, placed correctly, will lock the various floor plates in place. Once the perimeter plates are in place, proceed to the intermediate plates and studs.

The perspective sketch is, in part, conceptual in that the dimensions of the parts are somewhat exaggerated for the sake of clarity. Also, there would be more studs, for other than the ribbing provided by the upper clamping strip the plywood sheet is without ribs, the easy proliferation of studs making them unnecessary.

It must also be borne in mind that the ramp technique for the *Electra* set and the ramp technique shown on page 37 are not interchangeable. In one case we have stability through the creation of a large mass. In the other, we have a small individual unit which must have inherent structural stability. Nor is the ramp unit on page 37 suitable for runs longer than eight feet, and normally not higher than two feet at the upper end.

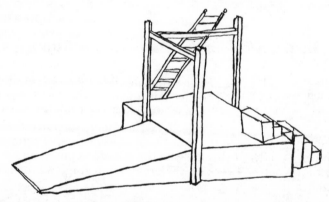

Above is a conceptual sketch for the beginning of a tour set for a barn interior. The ramp is clamped to a platform of lap-jointed, pin-hinged frames with top screwed down. Three posts are clamped as shown, and two beams added. Then some segments of the pier-type curved steps (page 31) are interclamped and added to the platform. The resulting rigidity permitted a working ladder to be leaned against one of the beams! [When clamping to the studs of a ramp some 3" C-clamps will be needed as well as the usual 2" C-clamps.]

Chapter 3:

The Arts Lab
or
Staging in the Style of
Store Window Display

The *Arts Lab* was my scenic studio in Shreveport, Louisiana from 1958 to 1986. It was there that I developed the greater part of my free-standing scenery. In the *Lab* I built many sets for touring and to the *Lab* I brought a miscellany of teachers and technicians for training. I also conducted similar workshops "in the field," a marvelous expression meaning somewhere else than one's homebase and where tools and supplies may be quite different.

I started thinking about the implications of freestanding scenery from the early 1950s. In fact, I clearly remember the day I was nailing base moulding to the flats of a box set when I asked myself: Why are all these pieces necessary? In a flash of extraordinary lucidity the answer came: To advance the set to the other side of the stage, of course! But it was not the simplicity of the answer that amazed me as much as the realization that when we work on the proscenium stage we tend to think *only* in terms of picture imagery.

All scenery can be classified in one of two ways: it either requires a picture frame to complete the illusion, or it does not. In the latter case the scenery is surrounded by space, thus becoming a "set piece," in effect, *freestanding*. A frame may be used to define the volume of space in which the set piece is placed — or there may be no frame at all: then the set piece is in "real" space be it that of a gymnasium, church, concert hall or lecture platform.

I thought, "What if the set piece could be developed into a complete scenic system?" I took the proscenium stage for granted, I suppose, because I was standing within one at the time. Certainly I was not thinking of medieval wagons or court masques.

I did not find a handy text in the library on the set piece itself. On the contrary, I discovered an absence of published material not only on scenery not requiring some sort of framing but also on theatres without fly lofts. This was nothing short of incredulous since there is an abundance of such theatres around, as well as much ingenious scenery to go with them. Apparently these theatres were regarded as substandard, and the scenery makeshift, tolerated until better days would come.

One must consider the times: These were the years when the arena theatre was growing; open stages for festival plays were being built; and television was skyrocketing — yet the imagery for "standard" proscenium theatres was still pretty much of a literal illusion (and a more costly one as time went by). Those who were experimenting with newer imagery had fled elsewhere.

In developing a complete scenic system based on set pieces I continued to work within the proscenium frame (which I still prefer for its singleness of audience perspective and for entrance and exit convenience). It was much later that I realized the workability of freestanding set pieces for touring and for platform stages where all sorts of activities take place such as concerts, forums, meetings and such — activities ill-suited for the confines of a proscenium frame.

A Central Esthetic

Around 1300, Giotto began painting pictures into which viewers felt they were walking, a style based on a sense of perspective and atmosphere, one which was to dominate painting until Cubism. It was this style which had found expression in the theatre from the Renaissance times by means of a proscenium frame.

There was no immediate counterpart in theatre similar to the volcanic arrival of Cubism and Surrealism on the art scene, possibly because the painter can put it all together in his studio and approval can wait . . . whereas in the theatre that small army of directors, actors, designers and technicians inch forward only upon the instant approval of a collective audience — not to mention that transient approval, one for another, among the artists themselves. Rather, change was to come to the institutional theatre in other ways.

My own revolt, so to speak, reflected fatigue and not artistic frustration. But anachronisms abounded! The advent of motion pictures and television with their direct access to real life environment had diminished the artistic force of literal stage imagery. The frame of the camera is integral to that imagery, for it is by means of the frame that the imagery can be projected to an audience be they here, there or elsewhere, present or future. The frame is not integral to live theatre, but instead an optional device, and one with a ravenous appetite for expensive spectacle. Furthermore, we now live in a world crammed with catalogs, ads, posters and prospecti, a neon visual shorthand. In effect, in our mind's eye, we are living in a world of store window display.

It is the store window which provides the keys to space staging in the proscenium theatre. Invariably, the store window frames *only* the space in which the display is placed. Objects in this space define the environment of the display scene, and these objects are "pivotal" rather than "peripheral" to the scene. This is the first key. The second key is the fact that an object in space is more abstract than a similar object that is framed, just as a statue is more abstract than a portrait. All we have to do is to compare the figures in a wax museum to mannequins in a store window to realize that the wax figures are the curiosities and that the mannequins seem more "natural."

Thus, in our store window esthetic, the proscenium frames the space in which the scenery is placed in much the same way as an art gallery contains the space in which the sculpture is exhibited. Of course, once the image of the art gallery is introduced the mind immediately runs to the "pictures on the wall." But the analogy can be extended to pictures as well and still hold true, for of "pictures on the wall" there are two groups: pictures that are framed and pictures that are unframed — and those that are not framed will be the more abstract ones.

We are now at the heart of design for space staging. To continue with the analogy of the art gallery for a moment, it would be questionable esthetically to remove the frames from the framed pictures without jeopardizing their credibility; yet, details from these pictures may be subtracted and reworked in such a way that the frames are no longer necessary, as with those metal sculptures that are so popular nowadays.

Scene Design for Space Staging

A SPANISH HOUSE

A NEW ENGLAND
SALT BOX HOUSE

The above set pieces illustrate three important points in space staging. First, both are in full *profile* and thus are truly freestanding. Second, both are quite abstract in that internal detail is optional. And third, in part because of the foregoing, a "reduction-in-scale" is possible whereas on the "picture" type of proscenium stage these units would probably have to be larger to be believable. This "reduction-in-scale" factor plays a very important part in designing scenery for space staging, for it is in this way that many pieces of environment may be brought onto the space stage that would otherwise be limited to the proscenium formula of "see-a-little-bit-of-it-and-imagine-the rest-of-it-out-of-sight," or, for that matter, the "cutaway" scenery of the 1930s which still looked to a "cyclorama of illusionary space" for protective atmosphere.

Two further examples: with the use of "props" together with profile, we can move indoors or outdoors without changing the central scenic piece.

From the foregoing it is obvious that freestanding scenery is essentially "pivotal," *dominating* the space about it as opposed to scenery that is "peripheral," which *contains* the stage (usually by running to the proscenium frame). With "pivotal" scenery the stage becomes the space in which the play is presented, and many interesting simultaneous scenic arrangements are made possible. In fact, many plays calling for complex set changes can be staged in this sort of space without shifting any major set pieces at all.

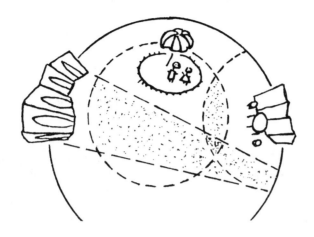

Diagrammed is a simultaneous arrangement of scenes for a play involving a weekend at the seashore. There are three scenes in all: the beach, a street cafe and a church. All scenes involve passersby in varying numbers. The 'varying numbers' of passersby suggest the placement of the scenic "pivots." The shaded areas indicate "shared space" that is made possible because the settings are focal points to which the actors *relate* rather than a series of sets, each of which would require a full stage.

In all this we are addressing the mind directly. There is nothing unusual in this. Take motion pictures, for example. It is assumed that film is "facsimile," an absolute reality. But the screen is dark part of the time. And the imagery has been chopped into "shots" that are juxtaposed without benefit of bridging. Yet the mind sees a smooth continuity of dramatic action. "What is there" and "what is seen" can be two very different things. Ask someone to describe in detail the setting for a play that he has seen the evening before. Unless this person is a trained artist, it is unlikely that you will get a very accurate description. You will however, get the meaning of it, the "intentionality" of the scene designer, so to speak, which is all that really matters. It is up to the scene designer to learn how to select the proper details and organize them in such a way that he communicates his intention or *meaning* to the audience.

When we read a book we may *see* a string of alphabetic letters, but the mind is not aware of them as such, rather, meaning seems to spring full-blown from the page. This is what makes proofreading so difficult. When we look through the rolling blinds of a veranda, the garden beyond appears complete even though we are *seeing* only a fraction of it. And when we look at a distant mountain, it is only distant because we have walked to distant mountains, so we know it is not as small as we see it, and that it would appear larger if we were nearer. The brain

43

is *predisposed to meaning.* I sometimes think the store window display man knows this better than the scene designer.

The Arts Lab — A Workshop Experience

As to the workshop program itself, when it comes to freestanding scenery there is need for a unique blend of structure and design not encountered in scenery for the proscenium theatre. For the latter emphasis is more on the "facade" and less on the methods of its support — that tangle of stage braces and rigging paraphernalia of which the audience is unaware. With freestanding scenery craftsmanship moves center stage. We have already seen the need for the fabrication of scenery whose backside is often as important as its face side. Furthermore, the audience cannot help but know that they are viewing "the whole ball of wax," and if ancillary bracing is used at all it must be discreetly contained.

Over the years I learned which of the many techniques essential to freestanding scenery were the more difficult ones to master and these I concentrated on during the workshop. I also discovered the ideal time for a workshop — 2½ days — about as long anyone on site had time for, and an ideal time slot for a long weekend at the *Arts Lab.*

I began with flat-frame construction and reversible folding panels — then on to the most difficult task of all: a flat-framed archway panel. Flat-framing was followed by some easier techniques — the "on-edge" construction for clamp-together slabs, including archways. Steps, platforms and ramps followed. Then decor by "dry-brushing" on textured fabrics. Any time remaining was devoted to starting a cylindrical object such as a tower. The rest, I believe, are easily mastered by following the instructions in my text, *Self-Supporting Scenery,* and viewing the filmstrip of the same title.

Chapter 4:

Stagecraft in Schools

Technically, a drama program in a secondary school can be a difficult challenge. A good program should include teachers from music, the woodcraft shop, and the art studio as well as the play director. Where such a team is in place the results can be fantastic, but more often than not the drama teacher must go it alone. Without the resources of the woodshop many of the techniques explained in my book on *Self-Supporting Scenery* will prove elusive.

Further complications are added by the nature of the average school "auditorium" with its emphasis on a formal proscenium arch and conventional stage draperies, though the working parts of a formal proscenium frame theatre are usually absent: a fly loft, adequate wings, a proper stage depth and an efficient lighting system.

All-in-all, the school auditorium is superbly designed for assemblies, ceremonials and pep squad rallies . . . and little else. An excess of draperies absorb music, the wide, framed space calls for realistic sets beyond the capability of the drama club, and an absence of spotlights makes selective scenery appear inadequate. It is no wonder that drama clubs prefer being squirreled away in spaces of their own choosing, such as abandoned double classrooms, or even cafeterias "on the run" where framed-up wall panels can make satisfactory settings which can later be taken on tour.

One of the first projects at the *Arts Lab* was the need to service an opera program of the Shreveport Symphony, with performances in a local high school auditorium — strictly an "in-and-out" affair from Friday afternoons to Monday assemblies. (The portable lighting for this project is described in my book *Stage Lighting In the Boondocks.)*

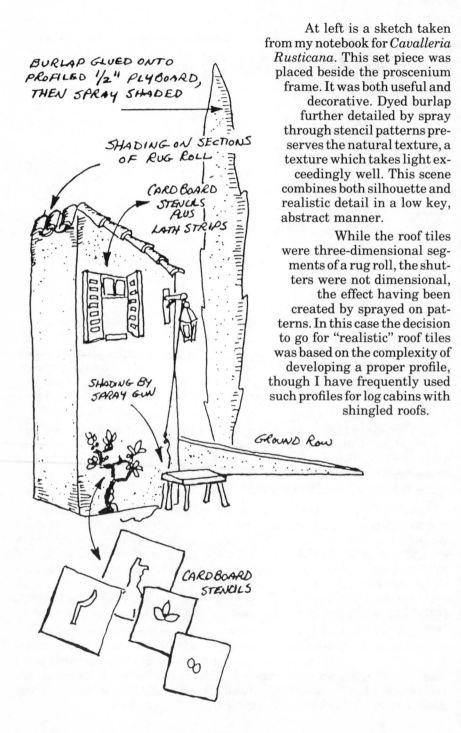

BURLAP GLUED ONTO
PROFILED 1/2" PLYBOARD,
THEN SPRAY SHADED

SHADING ON SECTIONS
OF RUG ROLL

CARDBOARD
STENCILS
PLUS
LATH STRIPS

SHADING BY
SPRAY GUN

GROUND ROW

CARDBOARD
STENCILS

At left is a sketch taken from my notebook for *Cavalleria Rusticana*. This set piece was placed beside the proscenium frame. It was both useful and decorative. Dyed burlap further detailed by spray through stencil patterns preserves the natural texture, a texture which takes light exceedingly well. This scene combines both silhouette and realistic detail in a low key, abstract manner.

While the roof tiles were three-dimensional segments of a rug roll, the shutters were not dimensional, the effect having been created by sprayed on patterns. In this case the decision to go for "realistic" roof tiles was based on the complexity of developing a proper profile, though I have frequently used such profiles for log cabins with shingled roofs.

46

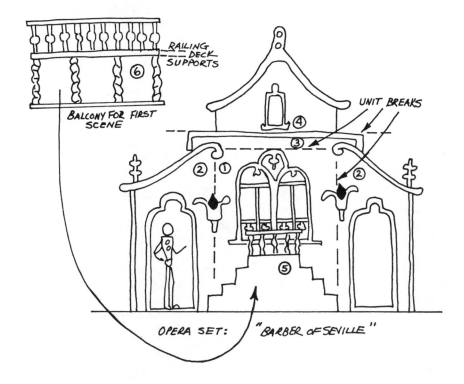

This unit set consisted of a clamp-together slab facade with platforms made of lap-jointed frames clamped fore and aft, thus enabling the entrance through the French windows. For the first scene a working balcony replaces the "decorator" steps (5). Hidden from view are two "slab" vertical stiffeners which are interclamped to (2) (1) (3) and (4).

School Auditoriums

This was also the time when the "baby-boomers" of the post World War II years were maturing into school children and new school construction hit an all-time high. Efficient assembly spaces were needed. One viable solution which took into account the multiple program of concerts, meetings, roving TV cameras and plays (that "all in one sort of space") was that of the open platform — that is, provided scenery for the drama is truly freestanding, which is much the same thing as building scenery in the spirit of "fly-by-night" touring!

47

One of the more successful solutions was an assembly area for a senior high school whose overall program was deeply committed to community affairs in addition to the usual run of school activities. A thumbnail "section" and "plan" are shown below.

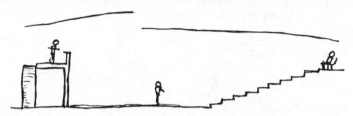

There are times when a series of programs are better served by designing both the platform and surrounding access at a common or ground level. However, it is essential that the performance area be *distinguished* from the area immediately surrounding it by a different floor treatment, otherwise actors will appear lost in space. In this example, both the wood floor *and* the carpet are laid on a concrete base, with the floor about ½" higher, and with a special nosing piece all around for the transition to carpet.

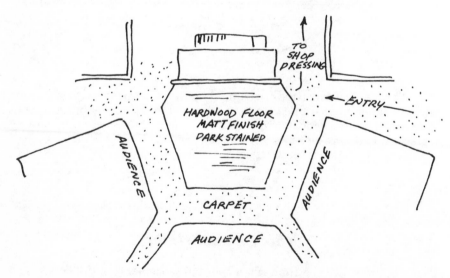

Such a space as this is created by individuals representing many points of view. Here the "corporate" client consisted of the school superintendent, the principal and the music and drama teachers, the architect and his engineers, the theatre consultant and an acoustician. These classifications are not frozen, and often overlap. For instance, the drama teacher might provide the necessary technical input as relates to equipment and support spaces, the architect might have an acoustician in his office and the engineering phases farmed out to a separate firm.

With this design, general circulation has been freed up: the audience has instant access to the presentational area, and wheel chairs are easily accommodated. Spectators and participants share a common acoustical envelope. On the other hand, an irrevocable commitment to freestanding scenery has been made and, if necessary, a training program should be available.

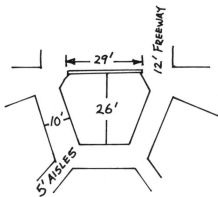

Our project easily falls within the guidelines for playing space dimensions described on page 72. The freestanding wall serves educationally for motion pictures and classroom overhead projectors but is keyed to an overhead scenic projection system located in the ceiling. For full details on this system see my book *Stage Lighting In the Boondocks*.

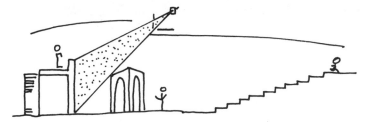

Along with a proper viewing angle and a pleasantly sized performance area comes the generally accepted spectator to performance distance of 50 feet beyond which the subtleties of expression go unperceived. Here the seating capacity is just over 400.

A Workshop Experience

Of school workshops there are two kinds: one in the studio of the artist, the other on site. There are both advantages and disadvantages to either.

On site you are in the space with which you are concerned and both the teacher and students can benefit from the instruction. The supply list for materials has been checked against local supply sources and the tools you need are either at hand or demonstrably absent. And items made during the workshop can be put to use right on the spot. On the down side are the inevitable conflicts of schedule: students leaving for other classes, the drama teacher running off to satisfy endless administrative details, reluctant cooperation on the part of the manual arts teacher who considers any invasion of his bailiwick with the utmost suspicion. Then there is the hasty departure of the busses en masse when the school day is over. At one school, due to a shortage of salary funds, the academic day had been shortened, and by three the school was deserted; there was nought to do but return to the motel and await another dawn.

In the artist's own studio the teacher is "on holiday," and there is nothing to interfere with total concentration. Here, the artists usually wears out first. However, the right sort of tools and supplies are on hand. Items built during the workshop make excellent displays for future workshops though they are usually pressed into service for local projects long before their "museum" days arrive.

Once in a while a teacher is able to bring a group of her students to the private studio. While this may turn an "in-depth" session into a free-for-all, often the group is able to build enough scenery to do them some good back home, in which case a U-Haul™ can be rented to transport the bonanza off premises.

In the fall of 1972 I spent three months in England giving a series of school workshops in freestanding scenery under the sponsorship of British Drama Advisors. It was an interesting experience in many ways. Unfortunately it was the time that yardsticks were being jettisoned for metric measures! Other difficulties involved the use of unfamiliar materials and the "dearness" of wood (Sherwood Forest having been long ago decimated, with supplies coming in from Russia and Canada). Time was also precious for a great part of it was constantly consumed by the endless round of tea-and-biscuit breaks. There was even time for a run to the local pub after the lunch had been served.

In the more remote rural schools folding screen sets using the reversible cloth flap hinge were immensely popular, for with these complete settings could be accomplished in an assembly hall. But as I worked my way closer to London the enthusiasm for my freewheeling concepts waned. Overall, Britain is still firmly wedded to the "prosc arch," as they called it, and if one wasn't available a "fit-up" was the next best thing. Now a "fit-up" is a giant, though temporary, scaffolding from which all the usual curtains of the proscenium stage can be hung. And now that the Christmas season with its traditional pantomimes was approaching, "fit-ups" were springing up all over the place. I recall walking past one in a

50

partial state of erection and hearing my companion, in a state of disbelief, remark, "Is it this that you've been telling us we don't need?"

Unfortunately, no matter where you are, the same customs and prejudices hold true: the "haves" are seldom interested in the ingenuity of the more poverty stricken while the "have-nots" work overtime with equally successful though often unpublicized "alternate" solutions. My *Stage Lighting In the Boondocks* addresses much the same situation.

Chapter 5:

Staging in the Church

Platforms in the Church

There is such a variety of church architecture that without prior reconnaissance it is impossible to predict what may be encountered. Some modern churches are built like open stage theatres, and dramatic fare requires little more than standard self-supporting scenery. In a vast majority of churches, however, steps and separating devices such as railings and choir divisions make some sort of platforming indispensable if only to arrange a proper focus in a sea of highly articulate, surrounding architecture.

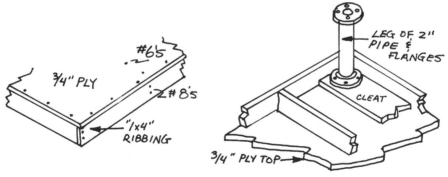

A tried-and-true method of dealing with architectural separations on tour are pipe-and-flange platform solutions with a wide variety of available parts in stock. Here we have a system where platforms are essentially "levels on sticks" and flexible facings will be needed. Velcro

53

attachments work well. I like a quality fabric such as velveteen — dark brown makes a marvelous facing where woodwork is nearby. You will also need a supply of flattish wedge-shaped shims to level the platforms properly. Flange castings and threadings are notoriously irregular.

My first encounter with staging in a sanctuary came with witnessing the "men of the church" attempt a wrapping paper surround of Jerusalem across the walls and other enveloping architecture. Secretly, I thought the central placement of some single scenic piece, a "symbol" *in media res,* might be more successful than an ersatz "cyclorama." So on the following Yuletide I timidly voiced my thought and in short order was catapulted down the central aisle of church theatricals!

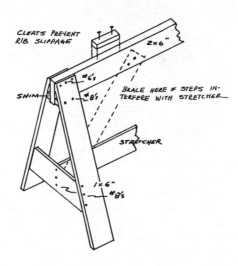

In this particular church a permanent dais with railing was easily vaulted, and sawhorse-and-platform elevations worked well. My favorite piece of scenery was a tower I had built for *Rapunzel.* Out of the tower I made an inn and to the tower I attached a stable with manger.

After some years as the "golden boy" of festivals, my daughters selected another choir more to their liking and I found myself within the fold of the Anglican Communion and in a "cathedral" instead of a Colonial meeting house. For a time I zealously guarded my newly found freedom from church theatricals — all the more so when I observed another "man of the church" amassing sufficient sheets of plywood to lay over a marvelous slate floor in order to anchor stage screws for the bracing of conventional "flats." But my reputation had preceded me, and finally the choirmaster asked if I would help stage some theatricals. I demurred, pointing out the stage braces, and my low opinion of that sort of solution. But my new friend quickly replied, "Don't worry — that's why I asked you!"

They say that "practice makes perfect," and, since this was my own church, for the next twenty years I built a number of sets for theatricals as well as adapting many others, all of which involved platforming of one sort or another, for otherwise my freestanding scenery would have been lost in the elegance of the surrounding architecture.

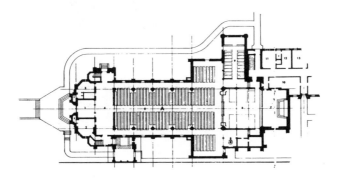

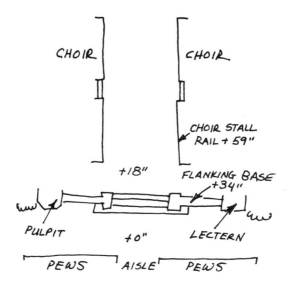

The church is cast in the form of the highly traditional "cruciform" plan found in so many Anglican and Catholic churches, a plan that lends itself to the staging of plays because of the centrally located open space (about 12' between the choir rails), with communion rail and altar well beyond the area needed for dramatic activity. This sort of plan favors processionals from three directions, which become actors' routes as well,

55

not to mention the excellent positions for side lighting from the transepts.

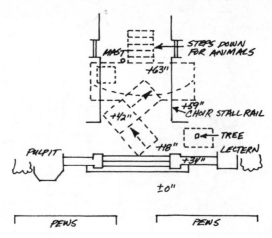

My first production in the church was a set for an opera by Benjamin Britten, *Noye's Fludde*. Since Noah and his family were principal singers throughout it was necessary to provide some sort of setting which would leave Noah and his family in full view throughout the voyage. Also the animals had to enter the ark. So the basic set consisted of a 4x16' platform (built of two 4x8' sheets of ¾" ply supported both by the choir rails and some sawhorses between). Because of the limited space the platform was mounted by means of a switchback ramp system. A set of steps to the rear provided the exit for the animals, supposedly into the interior of the ark. The plan shows how the ramp system was notched into the platform. The dashed line indicates the position of some gunwale units brought in during the "building of the ark." The platform, ramps and steps were in place before the audience entered the church.

A thumbnail sketch shows the ramp and platform in place. The first

56

ramp is a complete unit. The landing is of pin-hinged, lap-jointed frames. The top ramp is free-floating and bolted in place. Substructure masking was by brown velveteen matching the woodwork.

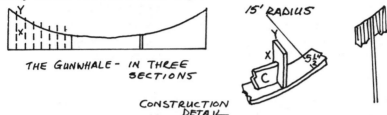

THE GUNWHALE - IN THREE SECTIONS

/5' RADIUS

CONSTRUCTION DETAIL

Rather than the usual "biblical" ersatz, the opera was cast in a Medieval mode. As the dramatic action commences, the village scoffers are watching the construction of the ark. Socketed into the small platform near the lectern is a tree made of a burlap-wrapped rug tube with a top disc and streamers of green burlap. One of Noah's children pretends to cut down the tree and it is passed over the platform to stagehands concealed below. Later, a mast similar to the tree trunk, complete with lantern, pulley and halyard, is set in place. The pilot's house, a fourfold, is handed up from behind the platform and is pin-hinged together. The roof piece, a pyramidal fourfold, is added. Two of the three gunwales are clamped in place. A spar is connected to the halyard and a sail is raised. The center gunwale is added after the animals have entered the ark. Black-clad stagehands attach a sparkling blue cloth to the gunwales and spread the cloth over the ramps.

Some construction details for the gunwales are shown above. The top rail was achieved by bending a thin plywood sheet onto the vertical studs and then trimming to shape.

The traditional rainbow took the form of a giant banner of multicolored silk strips carried down the center aisle.

Over the years I managed to get many of my favorite sets into the

church. The set for the Everyman Player's *Pilgrim's Progress* was "shoe-horned" in by exchanging the first three steps on each side. Then, since circulation was still restricted, I added some additional steps to the rear. The set adapted well to the traditional manger scene with angels above.

I inserted the *Electra* ramp by removing two sections which conflicted with the flanking bases. New legs were designed, a steeper pitch being dictated by the steps between the flanking bases.

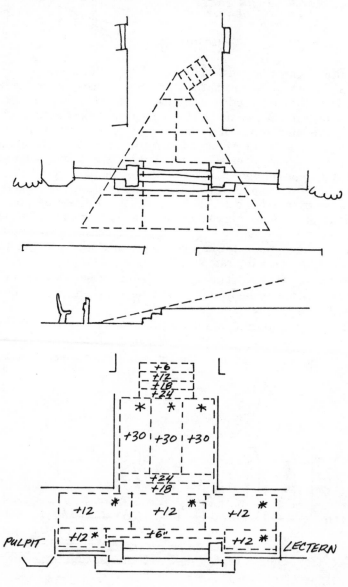

Finally, by dint of continually observing the immovable mass of marble, slate and woodwork before me during my prayers, I managed to come up with a permanent solution for platforming in this church, and, at the same time, an arrangement of parts which will pass through any standard doorway for storage.

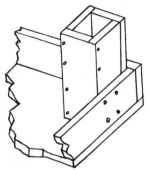

Detail of permanent leg construction for platforms marked with an *.

The platform and step units are identified by their elevations in inches *above the chancel floor* in order to simplify a description of the various units when used elsewhere than in the sanctuary. Let us walk over the units to get an idea of the levels. Ascending the marble steps we reach the chancel level and meet a solid-face 1'x12' step at +6" height. From this step we ascend six inches to the +12" height which consists of three 4'x8' platforms with permanently fixed legs plus two extension platforms 1'-9"x5'-9" that have permanently fixed legs along one side only and are bolted to two of the 4'x8' platforms. In order to set the bolts easily, cleats are provided to align and hold the extension platforms while the bolts are set, as in the detail shown below.

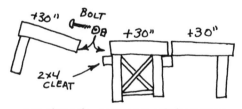

END VIEW ASSEMBLY OF +30" UNITS
(+12" EXTENSIONS SIMILAR)

The +18" levels consist of a complete two-step unit constructed of lap-jointed frames in the manner shown on page 28, with risers sufficient for masking. These lead to the +30" height consisting of three 3'x8' platforms. The center platform has permanently fixed legs (and bracing) while the flanking platforms have fixed legs along one side only (and no bracing). These flanking units are set on cleats attached to the center platform prior to being bolted on. All the L-shaped platforms are for more compact stacking in storage. Finally, a four-step unit, constructed of lap-jointed frames returns the players to the chancel floor level.

59

Some General Observations for Staging in the Church

The sight of a bunch of "gung-ho" "super-techs" descending on a church with all their paraphernalia can strike terror into the hearts of deacons. After all, to those of a religious turn of mind the church is seen as a holy shrine, and many technical practices which work well within the shelter of the "proscenium arch" or "backstage," so to speak, are unsuitable in a sanctuary, not to mention the Victorian notions of "life behind the scenes."

For this reason I always prefer unitary scenery that is fully free-standing, that is, not attached to the surrounding architecture. Since the church now provides the *overall* setting, any scenery, both set pieces and platforms, should be so designed as not to appear out of place within the sanctuary. Furthermore, all scenic effects and other equipment must be capable of fast set-up and "strike," so as not to interfere with the religious calendar, weddings and funerals. The latter have a way of popping up when least expected!

The Esthetic of Platform Design

Despite the growing number of places of worship designed for television, with their open platforms and slope seating, there are still a lot of traditional churches with flat floors around — and platforms are essential for good sightlines. I see three distinct approaches to designing platforms, along with their attendant steps and ramps, for sanctuary use: highly structured "scaffolds"; a solid mass of parts; or, parts erected "willy-nilly", and later faced with removable draperies.

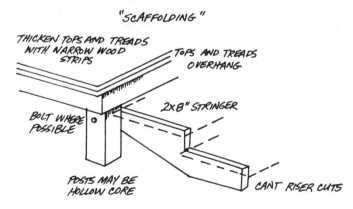

The stage has been described "as three boards and a passion", or "the unworthy scaffold", and though these definitions are more symbolic than literal they do set the spirit of theatre as something ephemeral and apart from reality. There are many instances in theatre where examples of impromptu scaffolding abound, from the little sketches on ancient Greek vases all the way to San Francisco-style rock concert carpentry. In this school of design, as suggested by the sketches above, one should feature a husky post-and-beam framing for platforms, stringer-supported steps from 2x8s to 2x12s, canted treads and irregular top and tread overhangs. The important thing is to maintain the effect of a temporary scaffolding no matter how elaborate the structure is. Scaffolding is no stranger to churches . . . in the larger cathedrals there is always some of it around, for repairs or mural painting, as in the opera *Tosca*. Industrial pipe framework is not recommended here because of ladders and the esthetic disparity of trying to join ramps and steps to such frameworks.

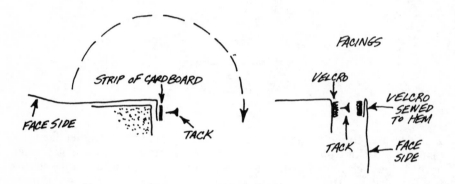

For detachable masking, velcro is the way to go. This does require considerable preparation, and if the detachable facing is only for a "one night stand" blind tacking is cheaper. A word of warning, however. With any facing that has a nap, such as velour or velveteen, you must make sure that the direction of the nap is consistent, not an easy task.

The Esthetic of Scenic Decor in the Church

One must bear in mind that adding freestanding scenery to the church environment involves an esthetic relationship between the scenic surface and the architectural surface of the church, for one is now the container of the other. For this reason, textured surfaces will always appear more "realistic" than smooth, hard surfaces, and dyed or "drybrushed" burlaps are preferred over painted muslin or untextured wood. Hard surfaces can be textured by adding some sand to the paint base. Where a roller can be used, roll on the base, sprinkle sand over it, and then reroll with a little bit more paint. This sort of surface is excellent for ramps where slippage is a problem. With "scaffold" construction thoroughly stain the wood — further brushwork is undesirable since it tends to soften the emphasis on structure.

Props

"Props" is a general term which includes tables, chairs, and stools, flutes, lanterns, banners and even certain curtains and backdrops when they are attached to the scenery by the actors themselves during the action of a play. Except for full-scale realistic room interiors, furniture and props always look better if built especially for the stage, and at a slightly reduced scale.

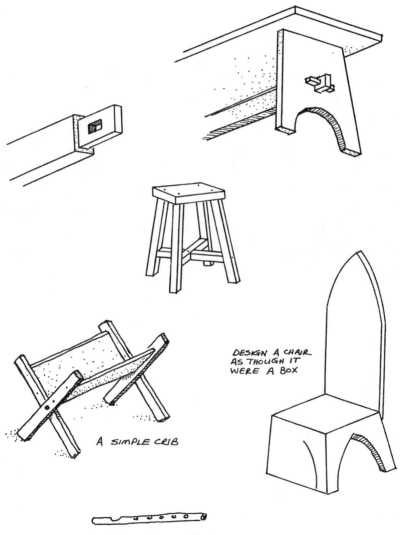

A SIMPLE CRIB

DESIGN A CHAIR
AS THOUGH IT
WERE A BOX

A SHEPHERD'S PIPE FROM
A 3/4" DOWEL, A DRILL
AND A ROUND FILE

A well-stocked "prop" show down the years will prove invaluable. Don't always be trying to borrow "the gifts of the Magii" at the last possible minute, but set aside funds and purchase likely items as you find them in second hand shops. Build that chair, table, shepherd's crook. Find those bent walking sticks in your travels. And don't forget the censer. Remember, "props" is a different world than scenery. A lot of hobby craftsmen who would shy away from platforms, sets and such will jump at a chance to make furniture, scrolls, lanterns, etc.

Lighting the Sanctuary Play

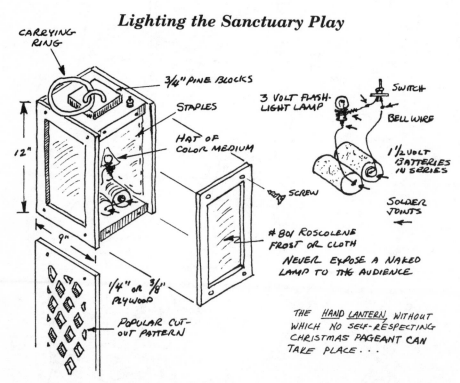

CARRYING RING

3/4" PINE BLOCKS
STAPLES
HAT OF COLOR MEDIUM
12"
9"
1/4" OR 3/8" PLYWOOD
POPULAR CUT-OUT PATTERN

3 VOLT FLASH-LIGHT LAMP
SWITCH
BELL WIRE
1 1/2 VOLT BATTERIES IN SERIES
SCREW
SOLDER JOINTS

#801 ROSCOLENE FROST OR CLOTH

NEVER EXPOSE A NAKED LAMP TO THE AUDIENCE

THE HAND LANTERN, WITHOUT WHICH NO SELF-RESPECTING CHRISTMAS PAGEANT CAN TAKE PLACE . . .

If asked for just one piece of advice in lighting a play in the sanctuary it would be: Use as much of the existing illumination; then, *and only then,* add what is absolutely necessary! Use the added equipment for *highlighting* over existing low-level illumination. If you take on the "whole ball of wax" you're going to need a lot of power, and power connections are not usually available in churches. The first thing to do is check out low-level lighting fixtures. Then identify the convenience outlets that are on different 20-amp circuit breakers. Each one of these circuits will deliver 2400 watts for a portable dimmer unit. And while you will not

64

see such small dimmer units heavily advertised it's surprising how many companies put together dimmer packages for a power supply from two separately fused wall outlets — it's just a matter of having enough extension cord.

It also goes without saying that soft-edged illumination is always preferable over hard-edged illumination — invariably a considerable amount of illumination will spill onto the church architecture, so emphasis will be on Fresnel lens spotlights, parabolic beamlights and, of course, the inexpensive and ubiquitous PAR "tin can" lights.

For further information the reader is referred to *Stage Lighting in the Boondocks*.

Section II:
SMALL THEATRE DESIGNS

Chapter 6:

Theatre Designs

With portable tour scenery "at the ready," Section II deals with some of the spaces our adventuresome players will encounter when they move out into the wide, wide world. With freestanding scenery, of course, they can go anywhere there is a flat floor, and with a sufficient number of folding screens, entrances and exits can be worked out. However, the matter of visibility remains, and unless a personal inspection of a proposed playing space is made some sort of graphic illustration of the nature of the space will be needed. Conventionally, this can be studied through architectural plans and sections.

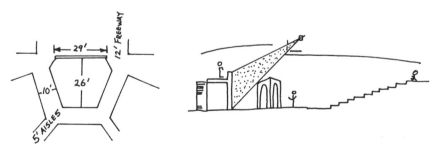

Shown above is a thumbnail sketch of an "open stage" assembly space oriented to performance. Obviously the sketch is based on scaled drawings and the notes and human figures indicate some of the important dimensions. To the left is a "plan" which shows the general layout taken from a viewpoint looking from directly overhead. The plan shows how much space is available for the performance, where the audience sits, and freeways for circulation. To the right is a "section," traditionally a vertical slice through the centerline of the building, as if a model of the theatre had been pushed through a giant bandsaw.

The plan also shows that a nearly ¾ audience surround is possible (our freestanding scenery can pass this sort of visual examination!). The section indicates a playing area virtually level with the main audience circulation area and exit freeways while the spectators are seated on pitched terraces. We can assume that the 5' aisles between the terraced seating blocks are stepped in some fashion. The theatre owner obviously possesses some projection device for illuminating the freestanding wall, but this can be disregarded for touring.

With these drawings in hand, a phone call can usually clear up any further questions. Without these drawings it would be difficult to form an accurate idea of this particular space by verbal description alone.

The subject of vertical sightlines is a fascinating one. Over the years I have collected data relating to stage heights in relation to seating slopes and the results are given in the chart below.

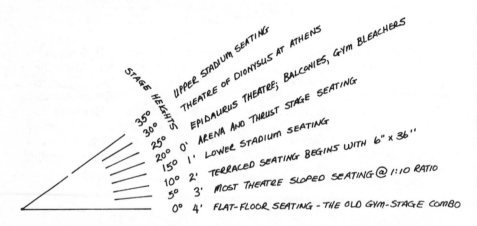

The problem of visibility has been with theatre from ancient times. Shakespeare used inn yards because of the many visual vantage points. About the same time in France indoor tennis courts with viewing galleries were also popular. Today, if all else fails, a large carpet unrolled over the gym floor facing a section of extended bleachers and the usual upper gallery makes an excellent playing area. The carpet does three things: it has a matte surface, it is acoustically absorbent and it isolates the play from the surrounding area.

From the chart we can see that having the audience seated on a flat floor means that the stage floor is above eye level, and it is generally conceded that an audience should be able to see the stage floor in its entirety no matter how shallow the perspective, and it was for this reason that many older stages were sloped upwards, thus enabling a use of the seating floor for other activities. Obviously these slope stages wrought technical havoc with dimensional sets and one doesn't run across them too often.

The section shows a "dished" slope. This is important because sight lines deteriorate toward the rear portion of any straight run (or equal terracing, for that matter). But when a dished slope exceeds legal ramp limits some sort of "landing" must be introduced before terracing can be added.

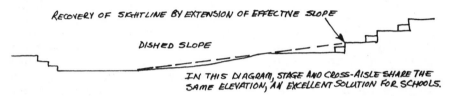

RECOVERY OF SIGHTLINE BY EXTENSION OF EFFECTIVE SLOPE

DISHED SLOPE

IN THIS DIAGRAM, STAGE AND CROSS-AISLE SHARE THE SAME ELEVATION, AN EXCELLENT SOLUTION FOR SCHOOLS.

It is customary to express seating slopes in ratios of so much rise to distance, such as 1:12, 1:10 (average) or 1:8 (maximum); while terraces are stated in actual measurements of riser to terrace depth, such as 6"x36", 14"x36" etc. Seating pitches are related to stage elevations, that is, the higher the stage above the first row the lower the pitch, and *vice-versa*. Also, the greater the degree to which the audience surrounds the stage the steeper the pitch needs to be. Sight lines deteriorate towards the rear portion of any straight run of slope or terracing. For this reason, slopes are generally "dished." But in changing a terrace pitch or in adding a terrace beyond a slope a landing is needed for safety.

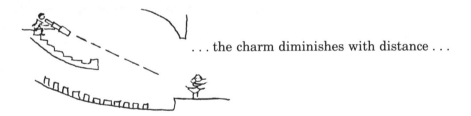

... the charm diminishes with distance ...

With any live performance, actors and audience are always in the same place, and this place is called a theatre. Thus there is a reasonable limit to the size of an audience. The charm and enjoyment of live performances diminish with distance. Motion pictures and television take care of large audiences more efficiently: the one by enlarging the image so that more people can see satisfactorily; the other by doing away with the need of an assembled audience to begin with. The charm of a theatre also depends on the audience *believing* that it can see and hear well. One cannot "prove" perfect sightlines by graphs — theatre engineers often ridicule the side boxes of the horseshoe theatre plan, but if the action on the stage is any good these boxes are invariably filled no matter how awkward the view.

As far a the size of the performance area goes, some theatres believe in building in more playing space than may be necessary, rather than run the risk of miscalculating for the future. While this may be true physically, esthetically it is *very* difficult to get rid of unnecessary space. I would not be going out on a limb by stating that, historically for drama, the average performance area has been 18 by 24 feet or thereabouts depending upon the particular shape of the stage. There are situations where the stage must be larger, of course, as with opera and ballet, and large orchestras, also the use of lavish, spectacular scenery. But by and large some 400 square feet of playing space will accommodate most dramatic activity nicely. The traditional Japanese NoH stage and the thrust stages at the Guthrie in Minneapolis and that for Stratford in Canada are basically 18 x 24 feet. Most arena (theatre-in-the-round) stages average 400+ square feet. Most "Little Theatres" have proscenium frame openings 30' wide.

Theatre Types

A particular theatre can be described by the nature of the audience and performance areas — their relationship one to another, and, in some instances, by the manner in which the scenery is displayed. However, there are such a variety of arrangements that attempts to classify individual theatres can be accomplished only with the broadest of categories.

If an audience completely surrounds the stage we use the term "arena" or "theatre-in-the-round." With the audience on three sides, America says "thrust," England, "open" stage. With an audience on one side only we say "open end" or "platform" in the manner of a concert stage. "Proscenium" indicates a stage with a similar linear seating plan but separated from their audience by a frame, like a department store window. An apron is that part of a proscenium stage, usually quite shallow, which extends beyond the curtain line of a proscenium stage. When the apron is very large, large enough for an entire play, it is often called a "thrust" stage. If the audience and the performers are arranged at will in temporary configurations with the help of risers and platforms the theatre is called a "black box." On the other hand there are "theatre rooms" which are fully committed architecturally, with permanent seating terraces, usually carpeted in the manner of "conversation pits" and facades with doors (and windows) for the use of actors in lieu of custom designed scenery. These spaces are usually designed for children too young for woodcraft.

Of these various types some will prove more readily usable than others for touring groups, especially with scenery, but in the interests of a complete survey, all the types of small theatres will be discussed.

72

Chapter 7:

The Arena Stage

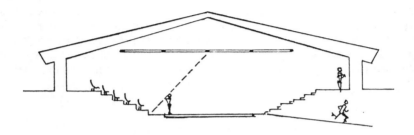

The arena theatre is one in which the stage is at center and the audience sits all around, hence the phrase "theatre-in-the-round." *Arena* comes from a Greek word for sand, which suggests that the stage is at the lowest level of the theatre — which it usually is due to sightlines and lighting spill. That the audience is not always seated on all sides is due to production demands placed upon this form which are essentially in conflict with it, such as orchestras for musicals, large amounts of scenery or extensive platforming.

The arena is included here for those times when a small production on tour can be accommodated by not using all of the seating. In this case it is important to know what in the way of lighting and stage movement can be expected.

One would expect highly symbolic plays on the arena stage since the space is basically abstract, that is, more sculptural than pictorial in expectation. However, one is more likely to encounter realistic plays, especially domestic comedies. The producers of highly symbolic plays have always preferred the romantic trappings of the proscenium theatre while the realists enjoy the luxury of the box type settings on the arena without all the trouble of putting up flats for walls. This is not to say that the arena stage has not been great at times for flights of fancy, but, statistically, this is not the track record.

An architect will draw you a circular stage because, theoretically, that is what the arena is all about. Besides, the seats fit better. A director usually prefers a rectangular stage so the actors don't get lost and the furniture placement is more natural. The problem of the bad corner seats which comes with a rectangular stage plan is resolved in part by placing the entrance ramps for the actors in the corners, though corner entry itself is of dubious advantage otherwise.

The majority of arena theatres are adaptations of existing spaces, and they work well for those who plan them, especially since these planners are invariably theatrical people. Few are built from scratch since "in-the-round" precludes lectures, demonstrations, film presentations and cinema.

While there is no common agreement about shape, there is remarkably consistent agreement about *size,* for too much space threatens that feeling of intimacy which led to the selection of the arena form in the first place. Even though the space requirements for plays may vary, it is better to be crowded at times than to have too much space at other times, for there is no way to get rid of unnecessary space in an arena theatre.

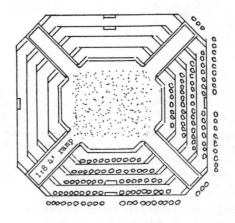

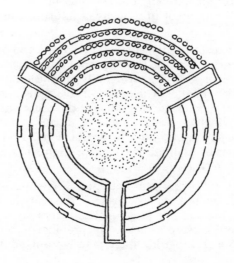

Two plans, one circular, the other rectangular, are shown on the previous page. Both have acting areas of approximately 400 square feet: the circular with a 22½ foot diameter playing area, the rectangular with an 18 by 22 foot playing area. The circular plan is the more compact, with 315 seats as opposed to 290. However, the rectangular layout has proven the more popular.

The angle at which an audience views the arena stage is extremely critical. Too flat a pitch and seeing is impaired. Too steep and the audience in the rear rows looks down upon the heads rather than at the faces of the players. Terracing is essential for visibility since the stage is nearby. Most codes limit step risers to 7" so 14x36" terracing works out well. Note that there are but five rows of seats on the above plans, but this is sufficient for the ramps to the service area below.

Lighting for the Arena Stage

One might think that the arena stage is not too far removed from the open platform, but such is not the case. For one thing the volume of the theatre chamber must be kept as small as possible for acoustical reasons, so the lighting grid is lower. Next, the directional axis of the open platform is absent and every spotlight must do double duty — that of backlighting from one audience perspective and frontlighting for another. Then, the audience is more compactly seated and becomes *the* background, so lighting spill becomes critical.

To figure spotlighting needs, plan for at least three spotlights (from different directions) for each 5'x5' area. Thus, 400 square feet divided by 25 square feet equals 48 instruments. Of these 48 half should be 6" Fresnels and half, 6" ellipsoidals. All the Fresnels should have the option of either high hats or barn door accessories. One third of the ellipsoidals should have four-way framing shutters. Another third, iris control and the remainder with pattern slots. Further, each designer should be allowed 25% more spotlights of his own choosing.

Note particularly the position of the first row of seats — on the first terrace — to avoid as much lighting spill as possible. There is nothing so disconcerting as suddenly finding your lap illuminated. Note also the *slight* space before the playing surface takes over. This is called the "gutter" or spill area and must be distinguished from the playing area even though it is at the same ground level.

The detail shows this relationship. And some acoustical considerations. Lighting service should be by ladder from below in order to keep the volume of the room down. It also goes without saying that because of the compactness of the space any extraneous noise becomes critical

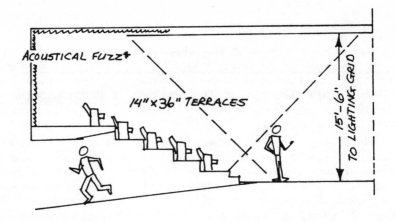

ACOUSTICAL FUZZ*

14" x 36" TERRACES

15'- 6" TO LIGHTING GRID

and, unfortunately, modern electronic dimming can be very noisy at times. This will call for additional expense for long conduit runs. And while arena staging eliminates costly sets the costumes and lighting cannot be compromised. The arena theatre is not inexpensive though it is still considerably cheaper than a first class proscenium theatre.

Chapter 8:

The Proscenium Theatre

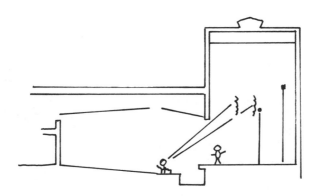

The proscenium theatre today consists of two boxes, as it were: the audience sits in one, called the auditorium or "house," and looks past a (proscenium) frame into the other box, called the stagehouse. Impetus for this arrangement came from the desire to have changeable "picture" settings. There is little sense to the proscenium theatre otherwise: the stage is too high for lectures and expensive acoustical reflectors are necessary for concert programs. However, within the pictorial tradition of the proscenium stage there is a noble heritage of design and a theatricalism which completely eludes motion pictures and television.

Scenery is the name of the game and provisions must be made for constructing it and for storing a great part of it. Just making the stagehouse bigger is not the answer. The stagehouse overhead, or "loft," is a high risk fire area and unnecessary storage should be discouraged. As for shop work, there is no point in expanding a high rise type of building to include a floor-based woodcraft operation.

There is one important point to remember about scenery for the proscenium stage: it is linked, one way or another, to the frame, and as the size of the frame is increased so does the scenery also increase in size. Even back in the late Seventeenth Century when changeable scenery became popular this point did not escape producers. A great effort was made then, and continues to be made even today, to shrink the amount of custom-designed scenery by the use of all sorts of neutral masking devices such as curtains, teasers, inner prosceniums, borders, wing pieces and the cloth "sky" cyclorama, not to mention "stock" scenery used over and over again such as woodland scenes, libraries, gardens, drawing rooms and bedrooms, etc.

Laying Out a Simple Proscenium Theatre

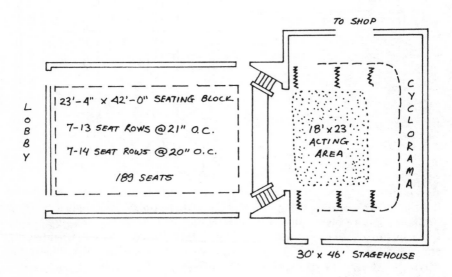

To SHOP

L
O
B
B
Y

┌─ 23'-4" x 42'-0" SEATING BLOCK ─┐

7-13 SEAT ROWS @ 21" O.C.

7-14 SEAT ROWS @ 20" O.C.

189 SEATS

18' x 23' ACTING AREA

C
Y
C
L
O
R
A
M
A

30' x 46' STAGEHOUSE

Most rows occupy three feet and codes usually limit the number of seats between aisles to 14, or seven from an aisle to a wall. A row of 14 - 20" seats equals 23'4". We would then have perfect sightlines through a proscenium opening of 23'. And since actors rarely perform beyond 18' in depth this would bring the seating to bear on an 18'x23' acting space, approximately the same as with the arena. The total stage area of the proscenium type theatre is usually much larger, of course, for scenic purposes. If we take 50' as a reasonable maximum distance for seeing an actor's face clearly we can commence laying out the theatre.

The minimum width of a stagehouse is double the proscenium width. There is no formula for depth. The best way to arrive at this is to imagine a drawing room setting about 12' deep, with large French windows opening out onto a terrace with balustrades. Add sufficient distance to the cyclorama so that lighting spill and shadows do not distract from the illusion of sky. Allow enough space behind the cyclorama for a crossover. In keeping with the *petit* nature of this playhouse, 30' would represent a workable minimum.

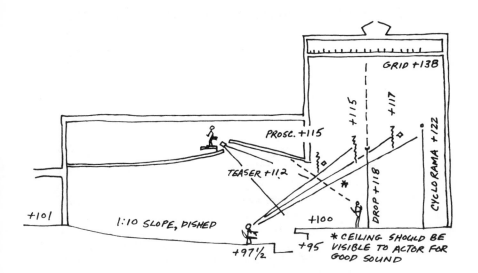

Since the best view of a proscenium stage is straight on, the main floor should be sloped rather than terraced. Using a 1:10 dished slope a three foot high stage is entirely satisfactory from the standpoint of sightlines, but a 2'-6" height is preferable for that feeling of intimacy. Sightlines can be improved by staggering some seats. This is accomplished by having alternate rows with seats of slightly different dimensions.

Next is the matter of the proscenium height. This could be a tug-of-war between what looks right architecturally relative to the auditorium and what works best for the overhead masking in the stagehouse. Usually the architect solves this in terms of the auditorium while the stage designer adds an adjustable cloth teaser for his working trim.

A typical masking system is shown using three teasers. These are so arranged that lighting is not unduly restricted yet the overhead area is sufficiently screened from view. In setting the height of the grid, or beams to which the rigging blocks are secured, two operations must be checked: can a drop in the middle position be flown out of sight; and can the cyclorama be raised high enough to permit the flats for room sets, etc. to pass under?

With the modest 23' proscenium rope rigging and sandbagging is possible, and, of course, this is the most flexible type of rigging. Counterweight, hydraulic and electric winch systems all came into existence to handle the heavier loads which come with larger theatres. An elevated fly gallery for the pin rail should be set along the wall opposite the shop door so that the gallery may be as low as possible.

You may have already realized that the only problems with the proscenium mode have to do with *size*. Take, for example, a demand for a larger seating capacity. Making the audience deeper impairs seeing

79

and creates a tunnel effect. Widening the audience means adding aisles or changing to "Continental" seating. Continental seating increases the row-to-row distance and this, in turn, brings us back to the depth problem again! Also, with Continental seating there are some stringent side aisle requirements.

But there is a more critical problem with the foregoing. Even when the proscenium width is increased it is seldom practical for its width to match a wider seating. This means that the extreme sightlines come through the proscenium at an angle and the practical acting area becomes wedge-shaped. The net result is that you are required to dress and light an area considerably larger than the actual area you need for the dramatic action.

This technical linkage constitutes the "proscenium dilemma." Add a balcony and the proscenium trim must be upgraded as well as the working trim, both for visibility and acoustical considerations, and the same dilemma commences vertically. In all this rearranging the actor remains the same size and his voice remains of the same magnitude.

Lighting the Proscenium Stage

The big plus in lighting the proscenium stage is the fact that the audience observes the action primarily from one direction, thus many subtleties can be developed: backlighting is backlighting, sidelighting, sidelighting, and motivated lighting, such as sunshine flooding in through French windows, etc. is easily accomplished in a literal way.

The big problem, however, is caused by the juxtaposition of two chambers: that of the audience and that of the contained stage, with the proscenium separator between. With the scenery close by, illumination over the stage inclines towards the soft-edged whereas lighting well downstage comes primarily from spotlights positioned in or near the auditorium ceiling. Now it is essential that the proscenium frame remain a neutral separator; stray lighting falling upon it proves distracting to the illusion framed within it. Therefore, spotlights for the auditorium positions (usually called F.O.H. or "front of house" lighting) are usually hard-edged ellipsoidals with matting shutters. Thus, the downstage area of a proscenium stage is a difficult area to light, for there are two kinds of light brought to bear upon it, the overhead soft-edged and the angled hard-edged from out front.

In addition to the various ellipsoidal and Fresnel spotlights found in other types of theatres, we find a number of "borderlights," or compartmented "striplights" that are easily rigged behind masking teasers. These provide a useful general illumination in an overhead situation where there is no opportunity for mounting and distributing light from scoops. By the same token, the constricted space overhead makes my own overhead background projection system useless. The reader is referred to *Stage Lighting in the Boondocks*.

The "Good Old Days"

If there were sufficient proscenium theatres of a reasonable size — and properly equipped, there would be no need for much of the freestanding scenery we have been discussing. For an illusory image on tour for a turn-of-the-century town hall theatre or "opry house" the changeable parts were inexpensive to provide and easily transported. The rather ornate proscenium frame with its stock wing-and-border masking set up ideal conditions for a painted backdrop, one whose graphics could even include foreground cobblestones of an illustory nature . . . and if the drop could not be "flown" it could be rigged to roll up. And there were a variety of other equally successful scenic devices.

Unfortunately, there are not too many of these theatres left, at least in the public sector. Most have fallen victim to the frantic race to offset costs by larger audiences — which, in turn, further escalate the selfsame costs. This is a race that has been won only in the movies and on television.

Chapter 9:

Open Stages

With the exception of the pure "arena," the term "open stage" covers a wide variety of stage shapes that are not separated from the audience by a proscenium frame. Such a simple statement, however, is technically misleading, for murky exceptions abound. Furthermore, the theatre designer descends to an Alice-in-Wonderland jargon about which not even the experts agree. Architects avoid the word "stage" wherever "platform" can be used instead, for not only does the term "platform" suggest the combination of audience and performer in a single volume of space but building code authorities are rarely persuaded that the term "stage" does not include a "working stage" with its proscenium frame, wing space, fly loft and elaborate scenery.

A platform in a concert hall is the simplest form of an open stage — the concert hall itself is the visual and acoustical container. Access to the platform is designed for musicians and their instruments, including pianos. Obviously any freestanding scenery must be able to be passed through these same openings!

A more complex sort of open stage theatre is that designed for dramatic performance, where the design includes more arrangements for the coming and going of actors. The Japanese NoH stage and the original festival stages in Stratford, Ontario and the Guthrie in Minneapolis are cast in this mold.

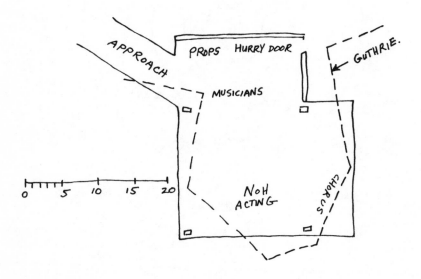

On this thumbnail sketch I have overlaid the basic plans of the NoH and the original Guthrie stages. The NoH has an 18'x18' main platform area (exclusive of the chorus area beyond the four posts). The Guthrie's tongue stage is approximately 18'x24'. It is not accidental that these areas correspond with the areas described for the proscenium and arena stages. Apparently 400 square feet or so will do the job for "intimate" theatres. As has been remarked earlier, it is difficult esthetically to get rid of unnecessary space!

Historically, a true open stage has some sort of architectural background whether it be a classical facade, the kitchen wall of a medieval banquet hall, "mansions" and "pavilions," a replica of the Old Globe inn yard or neutral, offset planes to assist with the stage movement. The audience surrounds the platform on three sides (or the better part thereof) and the overall style of production will be *sculptural* rather than *pictorial*.

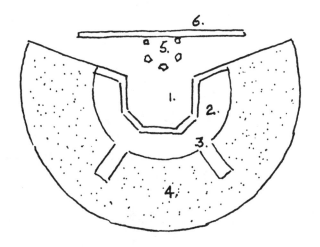

In the above diagram the open platform (1) is surrounded by terraces and a "moat" (2) which lead to ramped tunnels (3) that provide additional entrances. The audience (4) is seated on steeply pitched terraces. (5) is an optional "pavilion" providing inner and upper areas while (6) is the backing wall or some sort of architectural facade. These features are typical of many contemporary classic festival stages.

Often an open stage is "bastardized" by the replacement of the background wall or architectural facade with a proscenium frame and conventional working stage beyond. In this case the "open stage" is called a "thrust stage." Obviously, with this sort of arrangement, the sightlines are all wrong save for the most shallow of settings, though a certain degree of flexibility has been added, usually at a considerable cost.

Some dinner theatres use a curtained space to conceal a preset thrust stage which is rolled onto a free space after the serving tables have been cleared away. Such a stage is usually about 18 feet square and carries a scenic facade at its rear, through which actors may enter as well as down the stepped aisles. Comedy, melodrama and light farce is invariably the dramatic fare and the scenery is depictive, similar in construction to that

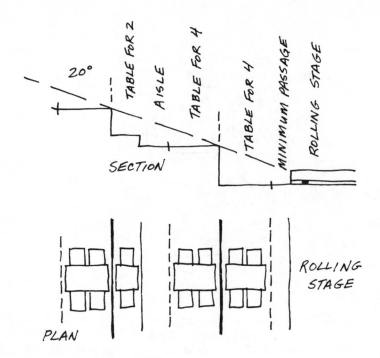

used on the proscenium stage. The audience sits at tables set around the platform and on terraces at approximately the same pitch as in arena seating. As in night club design, compactness is a virtue.

With the dinner theatre described above we are trading heavily on a feeling of intimacy. This same sort of intimacy in an actor-audience relationship transfers easily to "conversation pit" theatre rooms. These rooms are especially suitable for the dramatic activities of children too young to become involved in stagecraft which requires extensive carpentry.

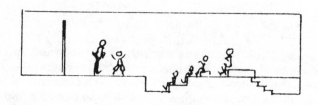

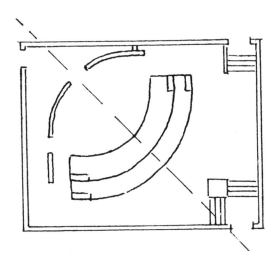

The plan shows a 30x40' room, carpeted throughout, into which some 14" seating terraces have been sunk. A curved freestanding wall, constructed with steel frame, 2x4s and bent plywood upon which Ozite™ carpet has been glued, provides a nailable surface for decorations.

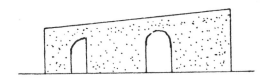

At the other end of the spectrum is the "empty room" or "black box." Such a space presents an interesting challenge since the less there is in the room the more flexible it is thought to be! The only installation that cannot be denied at the outset is a sturdy grid, preferably of Unistrut™, for the easy attachment of lights, scenery, rigging, curtain tracks, etc. Plugmold for the circuitry can be attached to the top side of Unistrut™. The grid should be about 16' above the floor, and extending to the walls. In the interest of complete flexibility the grid should be worked from below, so various types of ladders, scaffolding, etc. should be available.

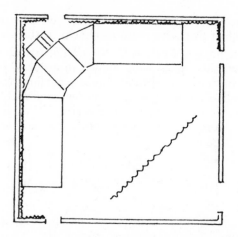

In such rooms it is awkward for the actors (and scenery) to be on a raised level so the audience is raised instead. Study the catalogs of portable seating risers before the room is dimensioned. Shown is the Wenger 32" deep, three-tier riser system in a typical configuration for open staging. From this study I would suggest a room no smaller than 40x40'. On the other hand, a room larger than 60x60' is impractical since there is a limit as to how high an audience can be safely raised with temporary scaffolding of any sort and still maintain flexibility, portability and reasonable storage.

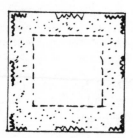 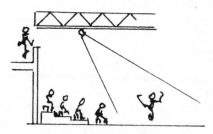

The acoustical characteristics of these flexible rooms are *most* critical. Carpet on the floor is recommended, of course. If the audience is generally located in one part of the room, then the area behind them can be fuzzed with two inches of glass fiber or two layers of loose velour hung away from the walls, and the area above them with acoustic tile, tectum or any good sound absorbing material. If the audience is to be moved around at will, then there is no permanent solution, though the situation can be improved by fuzzing portions of the ceiling and installing a continuous track around the walls, with curtains for 60% of the track length.

The clean volume of the room should not be broken by the introduction of control booths, balconies, etc. These should be in the form of galleries that are offset from the room as shown in the section.

On the first page of *Section II: Small Theatre Designs,* a plan and section of an assembly space were shown in order to illustrate the sort of graphic information needed to evaluate a performance facility. Every now and then a school assembly space gets designed without the forbidding proscenium arch, thanks in part to the roving TV camera and in part to the need for an assembly space where both the audience and the performers can easily mingle.

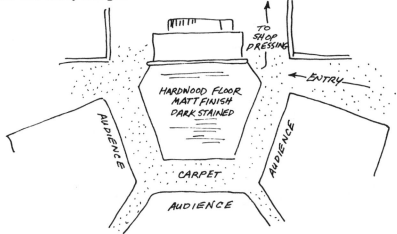

While the "stage" and the surrounding access area are at the same level for easy circulation, it is essential that the performing area proper be isolated *esthetically* — if not, both actor and freestanding scenery will appear isolated in too large a space. This sense of separation is achieved by a floor of darkstained wood set one-half inch higher than the surrounding carpet. The background wall can be colored by floodlights and is suitable for scenic projection — also for movies and slides. Acoustics are served by a ceiling common to both audience and performers.

By and large, scenery used on open stages will be freestanding in nature, that is, as set pieces rather than complete sets in proscenium frame style. However, there are so many "ifs" and "buts" to such a statement that further clarification is useless. The main thing to remember is that if one goes about scattering set pieces in space rather than building complete sets around the acting area an open stage will be easier to use.

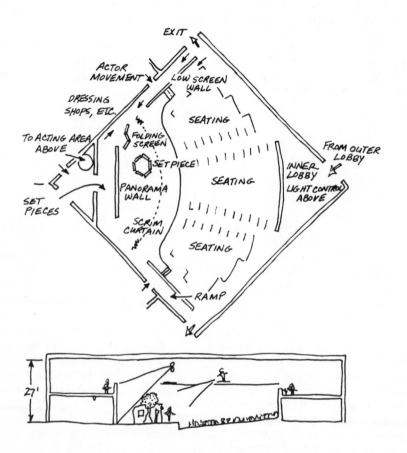

The above theatre, with its curtain track and side baffle walls, appears to approach a conventional proscenium in the plan view, but this is deceptive. It is really an open platform set at one end of a theatre room for there is no wing space or working loft. To attempt to use it as a true proscenium stage will be technically difficult. I mention this because of the frequency with which this type of open stage is misused.

Why is such a theatre designed to begin with? For one thing, the theatre is very compact — it is essentially a square some 90' on a side, and 27' high. For another, properly used, production costs are low, and a background projection system that is both economical and easy to use is built into the ceiling.

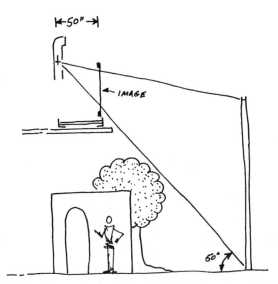

Another advantage of a theatre without a working loft is the ease with which lighting equipment can be assembled and adjusted by means of overhead catwalks. And in certain situations, especially where the stage is at the end of the theatre chamber, a background projection system can be built into the ceiling above, thus expanding the visual impact of the freestanding set pieces.

This system has no established name. It is similar to Linnebach in that it is basically a shadow system. It is dissimilar to Linnebach in a number of ways: the degree of clarity is such that a thread placed in the image plane will appear on the wall; it is inherently distortion free; and the image can be far more complex than a glass-painted slide. The best way to describe the system is by pretending to build one yourself, step by step. But first, you will need a sectional drawing of the theatre (or if you are in an empty building you might do it all with strings).

To establish the catwalk position on which the system is mounted, plot a line at 50° from the base of the back wall. Where this intersects the future ceiling plane (usually from 16' to 18' above the stage floor) locate the upstage edge of the catwalk. The projection lamp filament (preferably the 1000 watt T20/40 DSB Mogul prefocus base — the type used in a follow spot) will lie along the same line, about 50" away, as shown on the drawing. With another line connect the filament point to the top of the background wall (or the top of where you wish the projection to end). Between these two lines and at the edge of the catwalk, the image will be placed.

From this filament point you can also plot lines (or stretch strings) to the four corners of the background wall (or to the width you desire the projection to be). This will determine the width of the image. With some 1x2s build a light frame this size and cover it with some heavy paper.

The lamp and its base can be housed in a stove pipe. Cut a hole in the stove pipe for the light to pass through.

ELEVATION OF PROJECTION CATWALK

Now to make our first projection! The "elevation" drawing shows a small sailing vessel against some islands and a moon above. Cartoon this drawing on the heavy paper and make cutouts. Tape some yellow gel over the moon cutout, perhaps some blue gel over the island holes, leave the sail hole empty, and tape a scrap of chocolate over the boat hole. Place some moonlight blue or light green blue in a couple of the scoop floodlights flanking the image. Behold! A sailboat, islands and moon appear on a moonlight blue sea on the background wall. Some palm trees can be cut into the bottom of the image and covered with yellow green gel.

This is only the beginning of an endless variety of effects possible with this system. Imagery can range from tree branches lashed across the image area all the way to transparent dyes and cartooning on clear acetate sheets.

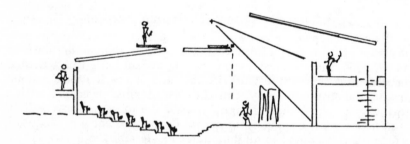

The reason for the clarity lies in a good *point source* of light plus the proper distance of the lamp filament from the image. My formula is:

filament size x 100 = lamp to image separation

Since the DSB projection lamp filament is approximately one-half inch square, we have ½ x 100 = 50".

The reason there is no distortion is because the image and the background wall are *parallel*. The reason the image can be made of just about anything (even paper) is because the heat from the lamp does not reach the image. The reason the imagery appears at all, and in different colors, on a background already illuminated has something to do with

92

a phemonenon known as "the persistence of vision."

Further details can be found in my book *Stage Lighting in the Boondocks.*

This same projection system can be installed in proscenium theatres where there is no working loft — in which case the necessary catwalk on which the image is mounted (and by which it is serviced) carries a horizontal masking plane below it. Upstage of this position, of course, all overhead masking should be in the form of horizontal or predominately horizontal masking planes the full width of the stage, since any sort of image projection system is incompatible with vertical teaser masking, the very masking which makes a working loft stagehouse possible!

Lighting for Open Platform Stages

I believe the open platform stage, especially where the platform extends well into the audience seating area, is best served with a "splashy" sort of illumination. Tyrone Guthrie was fond of the British "pageant lantern," which translates into the U.S. "beamlight," a fixture with a long-throw, soft-edged shaft of light. One of the most impressive light layouts I have ever seen was in the initial Festival Theatre in Stratford, Ontario, with 1000 watt beamlights, at a considerable distance and in a continuous arc about the platform, each on a separate dimmer.

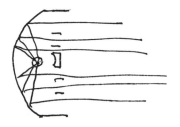

An open face beamlight with parabolic reflector. Concentric spill rings and often a small mirror block non-parallel rays. The absence of a lens permits a high light output.

For shorter throws the eight inch diameter Fresnel lens spotlight is recommended. I try to avoid ellipsoidal reflector spotlights for open stage work because their more precise fields create distracting patterns on the floor. Of course, there are ways to soften ellipsoidals with diffusion filters such as Rosco's Light Frost, Matte Diffusion and Tough Spun filters but this is a costly route to go. Obviously, a certain number of ellipsoidals are always useful, especially for pattern projection.

Decor for the Open Stage

A "splashy" sort of illumination is bound to include some of the architectural surfaces adjacent to open platforms. And many of these surfaces play a very important role in the dramatic statement a theatre makes. Not only do these surfaces provide a background to the dramatic action but they must also contain the arrangements for entrances and exits. The matter of stage movement beyond the immediate environment of a set piece becomes a problem which does not exist on a proscenium stage. There, one passes through realistic openings in the scenery directly into a concealed "backstage" area whereas one can very easily go through an archway in a freestanding pavilion and find himself right back from where he started — in front of the audience — that is, unless the plan of the set piece and architectural openings are properly aligned. In this respect one should study present-day architectural arrangements for toilet access in many airports where one passes through acoustically absorbent serpentine corridors. In fact, the exit problem for a deep thrust stage is so difficult that frequently ramped exit corridors are cut right through valuable audience seating.

EXITING THE THRUST STAGE

Acoustics

Up till now we have concentrated on *what* you see and *how* you manage to see it. Of equal importance is *what* you hear and *how* you manage to hear it. Since the eye is more adjustable than the ear the latter is the bigger problem — a problem compounded by the fact that scant attention is paid to the science of acoustics when, in reality, the theatre design should probably begin and end with an acoustician! Further, the problem of acoustics is twofold: that of distraction and that of clarity.

Sound Isolation

There is nothing more frustrating than interference from sound sources extraneous to the performance, for this is usually the result of improper building construction (with not much that can be done about it after the building is completed). The isolation of unwanted noise is one of the responsibilities of the acoustical consultant and it is foolish not to pay attention to his recommendations during the planning of the building, for in the long run, what may seem expensive additions to the construction are, in reality, basic necessities.

Some of the more common annoyances are: improperly mounted machinery which transmits sound through the structure, air handling machinery which transmits sound directly through the air ducts, too great air speed in the ducts, and sounds from other rooms, or from outside, which are transmitted either through cracks and fissures or by structural vibration. Special attention must be paid to the soundproofing between shop and stage if they share a common wall and if there are doorways.

Clarity of Sound

Some knowledge of acoustics is necessary in any preliminary discussion. If at all possible, a person knowledgeable should be present at *all* planning sessions, since the subject of acoustics is both a complex and difficult one. There is little point in going forward if you are not going to be able to hear properly.

Gymnasiums, empty stores, recreation halls, even large high school auditoriums are often used by dramatic groups. All too often in these spaces there is difficulty understanding the human voice. Any one or a combination of the following three conditions may be the cause: too large a volume of space for the size of the sound source; too long a reverberation time before the sound decays; and too long a time delay between sound heard directly and the same sound returning from reflecting surfaces.

Analysis and the proper remedial action should be left to the hands of experts. However, there are some precautions and corrections that a layman can undertake if he will remember Pope's warning: "A little learning is a dang'rous thing."

Electronic amplification is *the* answer to the problem of too large a space for the source of the sound. But amplification of an actor in motion is next-to-impossible without *both* sophisticated equipment and operators. Playmakers will do well to avoid overly large spaces such as aircraft hangars, abandoned factories, etc.

While some degree of reverberation time is usually present in any situation, the layman usually associates reverberation time with cathedrals. He is aware that music and chanting linger on — sort of rolling around from stone wall to stone wall. He also knows that it is hard to understand speech under these conditions and, more likely than not, he nods and dozes during the sermon. He also knows when a minister learns to slow down to the reverberation time so that his speech becomes more intelligible. The best way to shorten reverberation time is to introduce sound aborbent materials to the sides and rear of the audience area. Acousticians call this "fuzzing" a surface. "Fuzz" should be fiberglass board or blanket from two inches to four inches thick, or two layers of heavy flannel hung at least six inches from a wall. Carpeting is also useful. Halls with a combination of programs often have sound-absorbent curtains on tracks concealed behind wire mesh so that they can be extended for speech and withdrawn for musical programs.

The question of too-long time-delay between sound heard directly

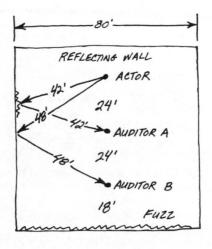

and that returning from reflecting surfaces can be illustrated by a simple diagram. Some experts believe that speech intelligibility is threatened when the *difference* in linear feet between these two paths of sound is as little as 50' or even 33' while others feel that 50' to 70' is more accurate. The point to be made here is the identification of a problem, not the splitting of hairs among the experts as to the precise solution.

For auditor A the path of reflected sound from the side wall is 84' while the direct sound is 24', or a difference of 60'. "Fuzzing" the wall at this point will be helpful. On the other hand, for auditor B the path of the reflected sound is 96' while the direct sound travels 48'. Leaving the wall surface reflective will help. It is also obvious that the wall to the rear of the audience should be "fuzzed" so that auditor A does not hear the direct sound at 24' while the reflected sound from the rear wall comes in at 108', a difference of 84'.

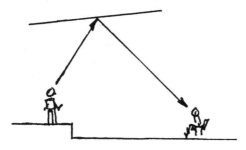

So far this analysis is based on a plan study only. To be truly accurate, a section should be studied also, since a properly located ceiling plane might so assist hearing for auditor A that the effect of the reflection from the side wall would be minimized.

Reproduced Sound

Since we are talking about small theatres with emphasis on live performance obviously vocal amplification is neither necessary nor desirable. And for the occasional weak-voiced lecturer there is the portable lectern complete with built-in microphone, amplifier and speaker.

It is a general rule that any sound effect or background music that can be done live is of more value to the production than one which is run off tape or records. However, there are times when incidental music and sound effects are too complex for manual solutions and some thought must be given to the provision for a simple sound system during the planning phase — if only to establish the location of conduits.

The diagram shows two locations for speakers, a temporary "scenic" position for a portable speaker and the overhead position that has been traditional with voice amplification. The latter position is always a difficult one to design into a building and nowadays regarded as passe, for, due to new habits in listening, there are other locations which work just as well.

It must also be borne in mind that any recorded sound must be of such high quality that the dramatic illusion is not broken and that the audience is not alerted to the artificial nature of its source. Unlike lighting, there are no "economy" solutions here, save the "home" arrangement of good quality units and component parts. With conduits planned for, many groups prefer to add the actual equipment after the building is completed.

Sound "on the Wing"

The reader may very well wonder what a dissertation on acoustics has to do with "fly-by-night" touring. The answer is: . . . "considerably more than he would imagine!" The foregoing has already alerted the reader to some of the touchier spots in acoustics — with a little imagination he may very well be able to remedy some of the worst problems he encounters, if only for a day.

Take a gymnasium. Perfect for freestanding scenery and some masking screens as far as visibility goes. Set up "sideways," on large carpet in front of the usual bleachers. Still too noisy? Try soaking up sound by hanging a forest of conical paper cups (or even egg cartons) upside down, attaching them to the trusses with heavy thread or grocer's twine.

With seating in a gym the long way with a high stage at one end, that's about all that can be done with flat floor seating. But if there is sufficient preparation time, perhaps several days in advance, very taut wires strung overhead between the stage and the rear of the gym will assist in the transmission of the actors' voices. And several layers of blankets across the rear wall will soak up some sound. The inverted paper cups to the sides will help too.

In a school auditorium, with pedestal-mounted plastic moulded seats on concrete, have audience members bring individual carpet pieces to cover as much of the concrete floor about them. If the seating is terraced, "fuzzing" the risers as well will be a big help although this will take a little more doing.

Some velour curtains are good items to have aboard. These can be draped behind the audience. Even if they have to be hung behind the performer this may be better than having distant opposing walls of reverberant materials facing one another with no treatment whatsoever.

In outdoor situations, panels of just plain ¾" thick plyboard set to the rear of the performers will help in projecting the voice. A "reflecting" pool ahead of the performers will help, as well as a cliff behind!

Epilogue

What I have written is a short book that can be read "all at one sitting;" a book that shows a pathway to low cost theatricals as well as a stagecraft that can be managed by a lone technician without assistance (other than a few pulley blocks when the platform stockpile gets too high).

It took only one book, George Kernodle's *From Art to Theatre*, to change my concept of theatrical scenery. I discovered this book quite by chance while browsing through some library stacks while looking for help for my students. Until I discovered this book I believed that stagecraft passes through some sort of evolution, growing better with each generation. Kernodle's view of scenery was diametrically opposite: that theatre styles share no such intrinsic evolution, but "piggy-back" helter skelter on marketplace art, reflecting timely values and little else. Thus, a strict chronology of scenic styles is fragmented into isolated solutions, mere products of a continually shifting culture.

Seen from this perspective I realized that much of what I was doing was by rote — traditionally-stepped rote — while the world was moving on. So I set about trying to add some common sense to my own backstage world and the economic shambles it was in. This book is the result.

Perhaps this epilogue should be prologue. It may well be anyway since it is my usual practice to read everything except novels backwards, and there is no reason not to believe others may do likewise.

About the Author

James Hull Miller, a graduate of Princeton, combines an academic background in literature and philosophy with many years of actual theatre experience of which twelve were spent in teaching. Since 1958 he has been a free lance designer and consultant. His field of special interest is the development of a new stagecraft for the theatre which takes the form of *freestanding scenery*. He has designed numerous open stage theatres based on this system of stagecraft for colleges, communities, student unions, schools and libraries. For many years he maintained a scenic studio, the **Arts Lab**, in Shreveport, Louisiana, where he gave workshops as well as constructed sets for use in a variety of spaces. A filmstrip on self-supporting scenery that was photographed in the lab is available from Contemporary Drama Service. Other titles currently available include **Self-Supporting Scenery** (the basic text) and **Stage Lighting in the Boondocks.**

Miller is a Charter Member of the U.S. Institute for Theatre Technology and in 1978 was named a Fellow of the Institute. He is a Founding Member of the American Society of Theatre Consultants. Presently he lives in Charlottesville, Virginia.

ORDER FORM

 MERIWETHER PUBLISHING LTD.
P.O. BOX 7710
COLORADO SPRINGS, CO 80933
TELEPHONE: (303)594-4422

Please send me the following books:

_____**Small Stage Sets on Tour #CC-B102**   **$7.95**
by James Hull Miller
A practical guide to portable stage sets

_____**Original Audition Scenes for Actors #CC-B129** **$9.95**
by Garry Michael Kluger
A book of professional-level dialogs and monologs

_____**Stage Lighting in the Boondocks #CC-B141**   **$5.95**
by James Hull Miller
A simplified guide to stage lighting

_____**Self-Supporting Scenery #CC-B105**   **$8.95**
by James Hull Miller
A scenic workbook for the open stage

_____**57 Original Auditions for Actors #CC-B181**   **$6.95**
by Eddie Lawrence
A workbook of monologs for actors

_____**Theatre Games for Young Performers #CC-B188** **$7.95**
by Maria C. Novelly
Improvisations and exercises for developing acting skills

_____**Winning Monologs for Young Actors #CC-B127**   **$7.95**
by Peg Kehret
Honest-to-life monologs for young actors

*I understand that I may return any book
for a full refund if not satisfied.*

NAME: _____

ORGANIZATION NAME: _____

ADDRESS: _____

CITY: _____STATE:_____ZIP:_____

PHONE: _____

☐ **Check Enclosed**
☐ **Visa or Master Card #**_____

Signature: _____
(required for Visa/Mastercard orders)

COLORADO RESIDENTS: Please add 3% sales tax.
SHIPPING: Include $1.50 for the first book and 50¢ for each additional book ordered.

☐ *Please send me a copy of your complete catalog of books or plays.*